Reading Fiction: Opening the Text

Related titles from the same publishers:

A History of English Literature	Michael Alexander
The Practice of Reading	D. Alsop and C. Walsh
The Novel	André Brink
Thinking About Texts	Chris Hopkins

Reading Fiction: Opening the Text

Peter Childs

palgrave

First published 2001 by
PALGRAVE
Houndmills, Basingstoke, Hampshire RG21 6XS and
175 Fifth Avenue, New York, N.Y. 10010
Companies and representatives throughout the world

PALGRAVE is the new global academic imprint of
St. Martin's Press LLC Scholarly and Reference Division and
Palgrave Publishers Ltd (formerly Macmillan Press Ltd).

ISBN 0–333–80133–4 hardback
ISBN 0–333–80134–2 paperback

This book is printed on paper suitable for recycling and
made from fully managed and sustained forest sources.

A catalogue record for this book is available
from the British Library.

Library of Congress Cataloging-in-Publication Data
Childs, Peter, 1962–
    Reading fiction : opening the text / Peter Childs.
        p. cm.
    Includes bibliographical references and index.
    ISBN 0–333–80133–4 — ISBN 0–333–80134–2 (pbk.)
        1. English fiction–History and criticism. 2. Openings (Rhetoric)
    3. Narration (Rhetoric) 4. Fiction–Technique. I. Title.

PR830.O64 C48 2000
823.009–dc21   00-053055

10   9   8   7   6   5   4   3   2   1
10 09 08 07 06 05 04 03 02 01

Printed in Great Britain by Creative Print and Design Wales, Ebbw Vale

To Fatima

Contents

Preface: Open and Close

This is a book concerned with some key questions in the study of literature: how can fiction be read closely, how might a passage from a novel be analysed, and, lastly but most directly, how does the opening to a novel or story relate to the rest of the narrative? Each of the 24 chapters that follows the Introduction to this book reprints the opening 50 or so lines to a well-known text and then offers a reading of that passage in itself and also in terms of what follows it. In brief, the aim of the book is to consider in its widest sense what it means to 'open' a familiar novel and provide a 'close' reading of its beginning.

The book is thus interested in ways of reading, and, to supplement the discussions themselves, there is a glossary of useful terminology at the end of the book and each of the 24 analyses is followed by a short further reading list. To an extent, the book overall constitutes a history of the novel, in chronological sequence, and illustrates the ways in which fiction has changed from its first English examples in the early eighteenth century to the late twentieth.

Above all, this is a book about how to read fiction, how to start to read a novel, and, most importantly of all, how to *reread* a text: to study, analyse and write about it.

PETER CHILDS

Acknowledgements

The author and publishers wish to thank the following for permission to use copyright material:

David Higham Associates Ltd, for the excerpt from *The Good Soldier* by Ford Madox Ford (The Bodley Head). Reproduced by permission of David Higham Associates Ltd.

The Society of Authors, for the excerpt from *A Passage to India* by E. M. Forster. Reproduced by permission of the Provost and Scholars of King's College, Cambridge, and The Society of Authors as the literary representatives of the E. M. Forster Estate.

The Society of Authors, for the excerpt from *Mrs Dalloway* by Virginia Woolf. Reproduced by permission of The Society of Authors as the Literary Representative of the Estate of Virginia Woolf.

Harcourt, Inc., for the excerpt from *Mrs Dalloway* by Virginia Woolf, copyright © Harcourt, Inc., 1925 and renewed 1953 by Leonard Woolf. Reproduced by permission of the publisher.

Random House Group Ltd, for the excerpt from *Brave New World* by Aldous Huxley. Reproduced by permission of Random House Group Ltd on behalf of Mrs Laura Huxley and Chatto & Windus.

A. M. Heath & Co. Ltd, for the excerpt from *The Road to Wigan Pier* by George Orwell, copyright © George Orwell, 1937. Reproduced by permission of A. M. Heath & Co. Ltd on behalf of William Hamilton as the Literary Executor of the Estate of the Late Sonia Brownell Orwell and Secker & Warburg Ltd.

Harcourt, Inc., for the excerpt from *The Road to Wigan Pier* by George Orwell, copyright © the Estate of Sonia B. Orwell, 1958 and renewed 1986. Reproduced by permission of the publisher.

Curtis Brown Ltd, for the excerpt from *Goodbye to Berlin* by Christopher Isherwood, copyright © the Estate of Christopher Isherwood, 1946. Reproduced by permission of Curtis Brown Ltd, London, on behalf of the Estate of Christopher Isherwood.

Random House Group Ltd for the excerpt from *Goodbye to Berlin* by Christopher Isherwood. Reproduced by permission of Random House Group Ltd on behalf of Hogarth Press.

Random House Group Ltd, for the excerpt from *Under the Volcano* by Malcolm Lowry. Reproduced by permission of Random House Group Ltd on behalf of Jonathan Cape.

Penguin Books Ltd, for the excerpt from *Wide Sargasso Sea* by Jean Rhys (Penguin Books, 1968), copyright © Jean Rhys, 1966.

Rogers, Coleridge & White Ltd, for the excerpt from *The Bloody Chamber* by Angela Carter, copyright © Angela Carter, 1979. Reproduced by permission of the Estate of Angela Carter, c/o Rogers, Coleridge & White Ltd, 20 Powis Mews, London W11 1JN.

Random House Group Ltd, for the excerpt from *Shame* by Salman Rushdie. Reproduced by permission of Random House Group Ltd on behalf of Jonathan Cape.

Henry Holt & Co., LLC, for the excerpt from *Shame* by Salman Rushdie, copyright © Salman Rushdie, 1983. Reproduced by arrangement with Henry Holt and Co., LLC.

Penguin Putnam Inc., for the excerpt from *The Buddha of Suburbia* by Hanif Kureishi, copyright © Hanif Kureishi, 1990. Reproduced by permission of Penguin, a divison of Penguin Putnam Inc.

Faber & Faber Ltd., for the excerpt from *The Buddha of Suburbia* by Hanif Kureishi, copyright © Hanif Kureishi, 1990. Reproduced by permission of Faber & Faber Ltd.

Every effort has been made to trace all the copyright-holders, but if any have been inadvertently overlooked the publishers will be pleased to make the necessary arrangement at the first opportunity.

Introducing the Text

'A beginning is an artifice, and what recommends one over another is how much sense it makes of what follows.' (McEwan, 1997, pp.17–18)

I

This is a book about openings: the author's opening of the text, the reader's opening of the text, and the critical 'opening up' of the text. In line with the quotation above from Ian McEwan, the chapters that follow this introduction are very much concerned with using the opening of a narrative as one way to make sense of 'what follows', as well as using what follows as a way to make sense of the opening. It is this double process that the book discusses by looking at the opening to 24 commonly studied texts, 22 of which are novels.

The difference between 'openings' and 'beginnings' could be considered largely semantic, but its nuances are none the less important. The opening of a text is its first printed lines, and these can generally be agreed upon. Even Flann O'Brien's *At Swim-Two-Birds* (1939), which famously starts by discussing how a book may have 'three openings', has only one set of initial lines; the linear arrangement of the text insists upon this, even if, as in this case, the narrator says that 'One beginning and one ending for a book was something I did not agree with.'

I say that the opening lines can 'generally' be agreed upon because nearly all books have what are called 'peritexts' – headings, subtitles, prefaces, dedications, forewords, and so on – which are arguably part of the text's opening and just as arguably not a part of it. Yet the opening of a novel is that which readers encounter when they read the book from its first page, and so is comparatively easy to define; whereas, as other critics have pointed out, the beginning of a novel or story is far harder to pinpoint. The beginning of a novel could be considered the first words written rather than the words that appear first in the final book, and they are frequently not the same: the first part of a novel written by an author will often not be the first paragraphs of the printed text, just as those first paragraphs may not describe the temporal beginning of the story that follows. The author's first idea for a particular novel (the genesis, so to speak) will rarely be the opening scene of the finished work. Furthermore, there is an added complication with 'beginnings' because everything comes from something else; the first pages of books often allude to other books, refer to incidents outside and antecedent to their own narratives, and draw extensively on the author's reading. The first pages always necessarily refer to pre-existing ideas, understandings and beliefs, such that, though they are in many ways beginnings in terms of the bound and printed book, they are also both produced and consumed within specific socio-cultural and linguistic communities.

If we switch from the noun 'beginning' to the activity of beginning, this again differs from the sense of 'opening' that I am using in this book. 'Beginning' a novel suggests that we are starting for the first time: we can only 'begin' the book once, though we can always 'begin again', but we can 'open' it many times. Therefore, I want to consider 'opening' a novel that we have already read, whose basic story, themes and style are already known to us. Openings are often undervalued when first read for the simple reason that they precede the rest of the text. Consequently, the reader is not likely to appreciate many of the references, allusions and images that are placed there. The linear arrangement of narrative, in terms of both a sequence of pages and plot, means that on an initial reading, the starting paragraphs are the ones whose significance is most easily overlooked, despite the fact that teachers often use the first page of a book for the purposes of critical discussion. Indeed, this is often precisely because the rest of the story need not be known when studying the opening. It is only when the book is finished, however, and the reader returns to analyse the first page that he or she can see how the opening works as a part of the text, as opposed to being simply its starting-point. So, by 'opening' the text, I want to suggest that this book will consider the first few paragraphs of a number of much-read prose fictions: the 'beginnings' encountered once again when the book is reread, and the pages deliberately presented by the author as the opening to a narrative which will in a meaningful sense develop from them. My intention is also to show how, by studying the first 50 or 60 lines of a number of books, the reader can begin to *open* the text up to a richer range of interpretations and meanings through attempting a close reading which starts with the book's first paragraphs but could then be continued for the rest of the narrative, opening it up further.

In terms of character, plot, narrator and style, openings are often meant to 'introduce' the text to the reader and frequently the first pages serve as overtures to the narrative they start. There are, additionally, theoretical questions specifically associated with openings in the same way that they are associated with *Beginnings*, as explored by Edward Said on the first page of his book of that name:

> Is a beginning the same as an origin? Is the beginning of a given work its real beginning, or is there some other, secret point that more authentically starts the work off? To what extent is a beginning ultimately a physical exigency and nothing more than that? Of what value, for critical or methodological or even historical analysis, is 'the beginning'? By what sort of approach, with what kind of language, with what sort of instruments does a beginning offer itself up as a subject for study?

These are questions Said explores, rather than answers, over the course of 400 pages, and I do not intend to rehearse his discussion here but merely to illustrate some of the problems attendant on describing the features of a beginning and to point out that some of them also apply to the openings of novels.

II

When approaching a piece of fiction for the first time, the reader should think along at least two lines. First, it is important to consider what is specific to the text, in terms of time of writing, genre, mode of publication, author, historical context, setting, narrative and stylistic devices, allusions, main theme, and so on. The more thought given to these areas, the more individual portions of the narrative will seem to have significance. Second, the reader needs to pay attention to the fact that there are features which all texts have in common, to do with the mechanics of language, which can be analysed profitably in any one particular piece of writing. Consideration of language in this detail is more familiar in the study of poetry; it is likely that an analysis of a poem would take into account such aspects as imagery, repetition and metaphor, but these are also qualities of prose and readers of fiction should pay attention to these formal features as well as to the larger issues of plot, character development, narrative style, or historical and political significance.

In the following chapters, the reader will come across discussions of several major subgenres and varieties of prose fiction; however, I would like here to introduce the two fictional forms that constitute the dominant styles of the novel up to the Second World War: realism and modernism. 'Realism', which is not to be confused with either 'real' or 'realistic', is usually used to denote a mode of fiction which came to prominence in the eighteenth century and shared much in common with historical, journalistic and biographical writing. Its apotheosis in 'classic realism', which was dominant in the nineteenth century, has been delineated by such critics as Roland Barthes, Colin MacCabe and Catherine Belsey (see Further Reading below). 'Classic realism' is a term used to describe the works of many European writers, including those of Honoré de Balzac, Gustave Flaubert, Charles Dickens, Elizabeth Gaskell and George Eliot: novels with reliable narrators who deal with contemporary social and political problems as well as personal ones. The principal features of realism (as opposed to the earlier Romance) are: narrative authority and reliability, contemporary settings, recognisable characters, representative locations, ordinary speech, a linear plot and extensive use of free indirect discourse. Realism is also characterised by what Colin MacCabe, in his *James Joyce and the Revolution of the Word* (1978), calls a 'hierarchy of discourse', in which the characters' understanding, of situations, others and themselves, is commented upon and corrected by the omniscient narrator from a privileged position of superior knowledge and general 'truth'.

Modernism challenged many of these conventions, particularly in terms of narrative technique, character portrayal, self-referentiality and linearity. Malcolm Bradbury has defined modernism as follows:

> Modernist art is, in most critical usage, reckoned to be the art of what Harold Rosenburg calls 'the tradition of the new'. It is experimental, formally complex, elliptical, contains elements of decreation as well as creation, and tends to associate notions of the artist's freedom from realism, materialism, traditional genre and form, with notions of cultural apocalypse and disaster ... We can dispute about when it starts (French symbolism; decadence; the break-up of naturalism) and whether it has ended (Kermode distinguishes 'paleo-modernism' and 'neo-modernism' and hence a degree of continuity through to post-war art). We can regard it as a timebound concept (say 1890 to 1930) or a timeless one (including Sterne, Donne, Villon, Ronsard). The best focus remains a body of major writers (James, Conrad, Proust, Mann, Gide, Kafka, Svevo, Joyce, Musil, Faulkner in fiction; Strindberg, Pirandello, Wedekind, Brecht in drama; Mallarmé, Yeats, Eliot, Pound, Rilke, Apollinaire, Stevens in poetry) whose works are aesthetically radical, contain striking technical innovation, emphasize spatial or 'fugal' as opposed to chronological form, tend towards ironic modes, and involve a certain 'dehumanization of art'. (cited in Fowler, 1980).

It would be misleading, however, to see novelists as suddenly abandoning 'realism' for 'modernism' in 1890: the process was far more transitional than that would suggest. 'Realism', for example, appealed as a term to many writers that critics would now consider precursors to modernism: for instance, both Henry James's 'psychological realism' and Dostoevsky's 'Higher Realism' were attempts to go beyond realism but also to retain a belief in the faithful representation of life. From the openings analysed in this book, it will be clear that authors from the eighteenth to the twentieth centuries have tried to 'represent life faithfully' in very different ways, and the rest of this study is deeply concerned with the methods they have employed in their attempts, be they realist novelists or experimental writers.

III

I now want to look at several significant aspects to close reading fiction which would be important to any detailed discussion of an opening. They are aspects to literature that are more often foregrounded when studying poetry and yet each is an important feature to consider when analysing fiction: the title, layout, allusions, the first line, imagery, style and structure. The first thing I will comment on is one of the peritexts: the title. Its relation to the rest of the opening is important: for example, does the title refer to a character, a place, a symbol or a well-known phrase? A significant distinction to consider here is that between the primarily metonymic genre of realism and the generally metaphoric modes of modernism. This distinction can be demonstrated at the level of titles: Dickens's *David Copperfield*, George Eliot's *Middlemarch*, Elizabeth Gaskell's *Mary Barton* and Jane Austen's *Northanger Abbey* are indicative of realist writers' preference for metonymic titles that are representative or social, using a part to represent the whole (the individual or town representing the populace or the country). By contrast, Joseph Conrad's *Heart of Darkness*, Virgina Woolf's *To the Lighthouse*, Henry James's *The Turn of the Screw* and D. H. Lawrence's *The Rainbow* are metaphoric titles which are not to be taken at face value in terms of reference or resonance. It is also noticeable in modernism that when an apparently metonymic title is used, its symbolic significance is particularly high, as with E. M. Forster's *A Passage to India*, Ford Madox Ford's *The Good Soldier*, or James's *The Golden Bowl*. Therefore, considering whether the title is primarily denotative or connotative is useful but it is also important to consider the range of meanings that a title could have, and how applicable each appears to be. For example, the title of the novel I quoted at the start, Ian McEwan's *Enduring Love* (1997), appears to be a reference to lasting love, but any reader of the novel soon realises that an equal stress is being placed on the other meaning of 'enduring': putting up with or surviving love. I might also add that it is important to check the novel's title on the frontispiece. For example, the full title to Dickens's *Hard Times* is in fact *Hard Times: For These Times* (1854), and the significant subtitle to Mary Shelley's *Frankenstein* is 'The Modern Prometheus'. Additionally, a novel, especially from the eighteenth century, may not have been originally published with the same title, and indeed with the same named author, as editions have today. For example, a book published in 1726 as *Travels into Several Remote Nations of the World* by Lemuel Gulliver is now known as the satire *Gulliver's Travels* by Jonathan Swift.

A further aspect which can be considered before analysing an opening in detail is the layout of the text: how the passage looks on the page in terms of paragraph length, typography, ellipses, dashes, and so on, as well as the narrator's use of such things as short or long sentences, speech marks, chapter divisions or headings. Readers should also pay attention to any peritexts. These can come in many forms and I will give several examples. The resonant epigraph to Pat Barker's fictionalisation of the Yorkshire Ripper's murders, *Blow Your House Down* (1984), is from Nietzsche's *Beyond Good and Evil*: 'Whoever fights monsters should see to it that in the process he does not become a monster. And when you look long into an abyss the abyss also looks into you.' Jane Austen's *Emma* (1815) famously has a dedication to the Prince Regent. Laurence Sterne's *Tristram Shandy* is preceded by a letter to the secretary of state, William Pitt the Elder. Many novels, such as Henry James's, have, or have had added, critical or explanatory prefaces. Mark Twain's *Huckleberry Finn* (1884) has a unique 'Warning' which announces that anyone finding a moral in the story will be shot. Lastly, the contents page is often revealing, as with Jeanette Winterson's *Oranges Are not the Only Fruit* (1985), which has chapter titles named after the opening books of the Bible.

Quotations and allusions are also important features to think about within the main text. These may be flagged by the narrator or may be submerged in sentences without any acknowledgement. The crucial point is that the reader should be alive to 'borrowed' or familiar phrases and to words which seem to be 'freighted', because allusions can be made to almost anything: contemporary events, popular culture, religion, politics, folk tales, limericks, poems or scientific theories. Usually, these are connections known to the narrator, or at least the author, but in addition any piece of text can be considered in terms of its status as 'discourse': that is, its use of expressions and terms familiar from non-literary contexts. All of these can be remarked upon because they indicate a great deal about the narrator or the characters, in terms of class, gender, education, ethnicity, beliefs, prejudices, and so on.

As with the title, there is only one first sentence and it serves as a prelude to the rest of the book. The opening sentence has a unique position, and this is partly why there are many famous first sentences to novels, but few second or third ones. The reader should therefore consider the effect that the initial sentence has. Does it directly give information about characters or places? Does it throw readers into the narrative as though they had entered the story in the middle? Is it in speech marks? Is it authoritative or hesitant, succinct or rambling?

Imagery is a crucial part of any text's effects, and comes in many guises and places. Significant imagery may be present in the title, or apparent in repeated references, or created through metaphors or similes. Every use of language which is not (meant to be) literal is a form of imagery and can be profitably analysed (very few uses of language are in fact not figurative). For example, you might consider whether the image has a relevance to the general subject matter of the book, whether it is an image from nature or culture, or even whether much of the imagery in a text is consistently similar (to create a particular effect on the reader, whether it be romantic, eerie or comical, for example). The most important types of figures of speech to look out for are metaphors, metonyms, personification, simile and synecdoche (see the Glossary for definitions and examples). Other features of figurative language to consider are puns, under- or overexaggeration, ambiguity, paradoxes and symbols.

Another distinctive aspect to any piece of writing is its style. Here the reader should consider the vocabulary and grammar of the extract, the tone, the ratio of narration to dialogue, the use of (especially unusual) punctuation, the employment of dialect, contractions, adjectives or adverbs, passive sentences, specialised terms and colloquialisms; again, in this light the reader should also think about aspects that have been mentioned before such as figurative language and repetitions. Further aspects to the language that might more commonly be considered in an analysis of poetry include emphasis (exclamation marks, capitalised words, italicisation), use of alliteration (consonant repetitions, as in 'seven sins') or assonance (vowel repetitions, as in 'bee-keeper') and rhythm (important when discussing a modernist writer such as Virginia Woolf, for example). With regard to fictional 'rhythm', E. M. Forster and his critics have used the term to denote the structural use of leitmotifs or 'repetitions with variation' in fiction which depends upon the idea of expanding symbols. 'Rhythm' then refers to the repeated use of phrases, words, incidents or characters to create a rhythmic effect in the evolution of a text's themes. The technique is apparent in Forster's *A Passage to India*, and in particular in the use made of the echo which haunts Adela and Mrs Moore after their visit to the Marabar Caves. In general, the reader should be able to register a wide range of repetitions and patterns in the text, at the level of sound, letter, word, phrase, image and symbol. Closely analysing the opening to a novel thus becomes akin to reading a poem and, for the purposes of detailed analysis, the reader can productively look for the same linguistic features in prose as in verse.

One more thing to add to this list is structure, which can depend upon rhythm. Structure does not just mean whether or not the piece seems organised, but whether it is discernibly patterned on a particular design. It is worth considering whether the extract builds up a picture (as with the opening to *A Passage to India*) or mimics other styles, such as a newspaper column or historical account, and even which of the five senses it invokes. Many novels, such as Malcolm Lowry's *Under the Volcano*, start with self-consciously cinematic openings, gradually focusing in on a particular character or event. Alternatively, Joyce's *A Portrait of the Artist as a Young Man* is a celebrated example of a text which imitates the linguistic ability of its central character at all stages, from Stephen's infancy in the opening to his time at university at the novel's end.

IV

There are four other aspects to the close reading of fiction that are less applicable to poetry and that I want to consider here. They require a little more explication because they are useful components of an analytical vocabulary and a specialist terminology: spatial reading, intertextuality, irony and prolepsis. They all apply not just to the opening of a novel but to a reading of any part of a text in relation to several contexts: the rest of the narrative, other texts, and the social uses of language from which the novel's vocabulary is drawn.

The concept of 'spatial reading' was expounded in an essay by the critic Joseph Frank (see Further Reading) and was derived from the idea that modern(ist) art is pervaded by a philosophical formalism that amounts to a 'style' (as opposed to nineteenth-century 'stylisation') which requires the reader to be more active and also highly self-conscious. This is mainly because of the text's complex construction, which works against drawing conclusions from any part of the book before the finish is reached. A parallel example is with land surveying, which is impossible from the flat ground and needs to take place from an elevated position so that all of a landscape can be seen at one time. The idea of spatial reading largely derives from cubism, which argues that a three-dimensional object or event ought to be analysed from all angles and not just one. Spatial reading is particularly important when looking at modernist texts that deploy terms repeatedly across their narratives, such as Joseph Conrad's *Heart of Darkness*, where a complex, rhythmical usage of words such as 'light' and 'dark' militates against any straightforward understanding of their meanings, which are necessarily always partial and provisional.

A second feature of a text it would be productive to consider is the social and cultural provenance of its phrases and words. When discussing any piece of literature, readers should consider influences, allusions and references to other texts. A different way of thinking about this is in terms of 'intertextuality', which, as a concept, acknowledges that a text is not simply the work of an author in isolation. A novel is the deployment of language drawn from many textual systems (usages from religion, the law, aesthetics, politics, mythology) in one 'weave', threading together strands of social discourses. A text is never original in the sense that the words, if not the expressions it employs, are to be found elsewhere (in intertexts), even though it is original in the sense that it is a unique arrangement of those words. Thus, when analysing the opening to a novel, it is frequently profitable to consider where the text draws its language from.

'Irony', which is pervasive in fiction, occurs whenever appearance and 'reality' differ, even though in a limited verbal sense 'irony' refers to a figure of speech in which one meaning of a word or expression clashes with an alternative meaning. In most literary criticism, intentional irony has generally been admired as a quality of textual complexity, but it is also common now to consider ironies in the text irrespective of authorial intention, precisely because the flexibility and plurality of meaning in relation to language allow multiple interpretations of almost any utterance. So, on the one hand, all language is ambiguous and has a plurality of meanings, and, on the other hand, all language is narrated. Who is speaking is always a key question, and it may have more than one answer. The opening sentence to Jane Austen's *Pride and Prejudice* is spoken directly by the narrator. However, it soon becomes clear that the view expressed in the opening sentence is not that of the narrator, let alone the author, but of Mrs Bennet. In other words, a case can be made for thinking that the opening words of the novel are those of a character, of the author (or an 'implied' author), or simply of the narrator. The key point is that when readers identify a piece of writing as 'ironic', they are asserting that it does not mean what it appears to, at face value, and so are opening up a gap between what the text says and what it means: a reading practice that, because of the ability of language to mean so many things, including the opposite of what we intially take it to mean, can be expanded to all kinds of interpretations that read between the lines of texts. For many critics, it is precisely this richness of narration and speech in fiction that makes it such a fertile and 'open' genre. For example, the voice of any one character in a novel will be a meeting point for all sorts of overt and covert discourses, or viewpoints, which will themselves be put into competition with other discourses and voices, creating an enormously complex matrix of language, in which stresses and emphases can be placed not only on what the text says but on what it does not say.

An understanding of characters' voices or the narrator's use of irony can often only be gained from reading the entire text, but it is knowledge that can be brought to bear on individual portions of the narrative, including the opening. A fourth aspect to narrative worth emphasising here is also best understood in the light of the entire text. 'Prolepsis' is the anticipation of an event which has yet to occur and is a particularly important aspect to the openings of novels. Strictly speaking, prolepsis requires that a future event be treated as though it is currently happening (for example, 'I am gone'), but, more loosely, critics use it to refer to allusions to, and foreshadowings of, later incidents in the narrative. For instance, the narrator of the first text examined in this book, *Robinson Crusoe*, speaks on the opening page of his narrative of 'the life of misery that was to befal me', explicitly placing current events and descriptions in the light of what has not yet been narrated. Prolepsis is a figure of speech which can be used either to anticipate some future incident's connection with that which is currently being narrated, or simply to create suspense, but it can also work at the level of language, where words and phrases themselves can be linked to future ones. Additionally, telling the story with hindsight, as with *Jane Eyre* or *Great Expectations*, is a common method through which narrators introduce a sense of a double-perspective into the narrative, speaking, to different degrees, as both older and younger self. A further technique to create suspense by introducing two time frames is to begin the story at its end, as Malcolm Lowry does in *Under the Volcano* with a prefatory chapter set one year in the future. Here, the allusions are to events which are prior in time but later in the text, and if the reader considers this opening to be 'the present' of the text, then the remaining 11 chapters constitute an extended flashback.

In conclusion, the features discussed in this section refer attention to the linguistic and structural aspects to fiction, emphasising once more that prose operates in a complex fashion which can best be appreciated in any particular extract by close attention to, first, its specific qualities, many of which might more often be analysed in poetry, and second, its relation to the rest of the narrative and to social discourses.

V

Lastly, I want to raise the question of the omnipresence of not narrators but narrative. To begin with, it is obvious that narrative is not exclusive to fiction. Films, television programmes, plays, songs and poetry all contain narrative. All of these tell stories, using images and/or words. The more difficult question to ask is: what uses of language, or of visual imagery, do not contain narrative? Does a bank statement have a narrative? Does the description of a scientific experiment have one? Do the workings of a mathematical calculation?

Though we would want to make distinctions between kinds of narrative, we would probably give an affirmative answer to each of these questions. All of these examples are concerned with narrative in that they are concerned with causation. They all tell stories by arranging events in an order, with one event followed by another which in some sense develops from it. This brings us to one important element of narrative: time. Stories tell us about change over time, and so does a bank statement: your bank balance has gone down because you wrote a cheque, took some money out, or had to pay bank charges, and so on.

More difficult examples would be photographs, or shopping lists, or telephone directories. Do these have narratives? These are more problematic because they do not usually deal with time; but even so, many critics would argue that they are concerned with narratives because human beings are story-telling animals. People will provide them with narratives when they look at them or read them, because they contain information from which it is possible to construct stories. Photographs often seem to tell us things about the people in them; shopping lists imply a great deal about people's lifestyles; and even telephone directories tell a story about people in relation to towns and addresses: a telephone directory is a structured narrative of names, families and genealogies.

Some critics have therefore argued that everything is narrative. Rather than think of stories as something peculiar to texts, we might advance the view that humans understand everything as stories. In other words, narrative is a way in which to construct the world. Even physicists explain their theories in terms of stories: Stephen Hawking's *A Brief History of Time* has been enormously popular largely because it has presented the most advanced thinking about physics in terms of a narrative: as a *history* of time and a *story* of the universe from beginning to probable end. Arguably, everything has a narrative: for example, even a cooking recipe has a plot in that it is structured around the idea of 'this, then this, then this'. Narrative is, consequently, perhaps not something we find in books or 'stories' but something we apply to life; and when we find anything in culture, and perhaps also nature, human beings want to ask 'What does it mean?', and so fit a narrative to it.

In other words, narrative is less a quality of things such as books and films as of readers and languages. Many critics will argue that everything has a narrative because human beings always make connections and form opinions: they think in terms of narratives. So, in analysing texts, it is important to remember that we bring our own narratives to bear on them. This can be unhelpful, if it distracts us from reading attentively and prevents us from perceiving the range of possible meanings and the many nuances within a text; but it can also be enormously productive if we recognise that all interpretation is a result of a dialogue between the text and the reader, and that the wider range of knowledges and narratives we can employ to support our reading of the text, the more robust and defensible will be the meanings we can squeeze from it.

There is no limit to what can be said about the opening of a text, and it would be possible to write a book about the start of any one of the texts discussed in the following chapters. It would also be possible to limit the commentary to just vocabulary, or imagery, or style, or any one of a number of other aspects to authorship or textuality, but this would be unnecessarily limiting and soon become repetitive. The fundamental conviction of literary studies, and certainly the basis of its continuance, has to be the text's abundance and plurality of meanings. For this reason, I have avoided repeating the same kinds of material across the different readings, and some chapters are devoted to a close reading of the passage itself while others also consider the opening in terms of a style, such as realism and modernism. What all the chapters do is use the opening paragraphs as a springboard for discussion, and I have taken care not to move on to wider discussions of the texts, their histories or genres without rooting such material in examples from the opening passages themselves. None of these discussions is intended to be anywhere near exhaustive, but I hope the variety of approaches and readings will encourage readers to add to each of them individually, in the belief that opening the text is the beginning of an analysis that should never be considered complete.

References and Further Reading

Belsey, Catherine (1980) *Critical Practice*, London: Methuen.

Bennett, Andrew and Royle, Nicholas (1999) *An Introduction to Literature, Criticism and Theory* (2nd edn), Hemel Hempstead: Prentice-Hall.

Fowler, Roger (ed.) (1980) *A Dictionary of Modern Critical Terms*, London: Routledge.

Frank, Joseph (1963) 'Spatial form in Modern Literature', *The Widening Gyre: Crisis and Mastery in Modern Literature*, New Brunswick, NJ: Prentice-Hall.

Hall, Stuart (1984) 'The Narrative Construction of Reality', *Southern Review* 17, pp. 1–17.

Hawking, Stephen (1995) *A Brief History of Time*, New York: Bantam.

McEwan, Ian (1987) *Enduring Love*, London: Vintage.

MacCabe, Colin (1978) *James Joyce and the Revolution of the Word*, London: Macmillan – now Palgrave.

Milligan, Ian (1983) *The Novel in English: An Introduction*, London: Macmillan – now Palgrave.

Nuttall, A. D. (1992) *Openings: Narrative Beginnings from the Epic to the Novel*, Oxford: Clarendon.

Rimmon-Kenan, Shlomith (1983) *Narrative Fiction: Contemporary Poetics*, London: Methuen.

Said, Edward (1975) *Beginnings: Intention and Method*, Baltimore, MD: Johns Hopkins University.

Daniel Defoe
Robinson Crusoe
(1719)

I was born in the year 1632, in the city of York, of a good
family, tho' not of that country, my father being a foreigner of
Bremen, who settled first at Hull. He got a good estate by mer-
chandise, and leaving off his trade lived afterward at York, from
whence he had married my mother, whose relations were named   5
Robinson, a very good family in that country, and from whom I
was called Robinson Kreutznaer; but by the usual corruption of
words in England, we are now called, nay, we call our selves and
write our name, Crusoe, and so my companions always called me.
    I had two elder brothers, one of which was lieutenant collonel   10
to an English regiment of foot in Flanders, formerly commanded
by the famous Coll. Lockhart, and was killed at the battle near
Dunkirk against the Spaniards. What became of my second
brother I never knew any more than my father or mother did
know what was become of me.   15
    Being the third son of the family and not bred to any trade, my
head began to be filled very early with rambling thoughts. My
father, who was very ancient, had given me a competent share of
learning, as far as house-education and a country free-school
generally goes, and designed me for the law; but I would be satis- 20
fied with nothing but going to sea, and my inclination to this led
me so strongly against the will, nay the commands of my father,
and against all the entreaties and perswasions of my mother and
other friends, that there seemed to be something fatal in that
propension of nature tending directly to the life of misery which   25
was to befal me.
    My father, a wise and grave man, gave me serious and excel-
lent counsel against what he foresaw was my design. He called
me one morning into his chamber, where he was confined by the
gout, and expostulated very warmly with me upon this subject.   30
He asked me what reasons more than a meer wandring inclina-

tion I had for leaving my father's house and my native country,
where I might be well introduced, and had a prospect of raising
my fortune by application and industry, with a life of ease and
pleasure. He told me it was for men of desperate fortunes on one   35
hand, or of aspiring, superior fortune on the other, who went
abroad upon adventures, to rise by enterprize, and make themselves famous in undertakings of a nature out of the common
road; that these things were all either too far above me, or too
far below me; that mine was the middle state, or what might be   40
called the upper station of low life, which he had found by long
experience was the best state in the world, the most suited to
human happiness, not exposed to the miseries and hardships, the
labour and sufferings of the mechanick part of mankind, and not
embarrassed with the pride, luxury, ambition, and envy of the   45
upper part of mankind. He told me I might judge of the happiness of this state by this one thing, viz. that this was the state of
life which all other people envied, that kings have frequently
lamented the miserable consequences of being born to great
things, and wished they had been placed in the middle of the   50
two extremes, between the mean and the great; that the wise
man gave his testinmony to this as the just standard of true
felicity, when he prayed to have neither poverty or riches.

                                        (Harmondsworth: Penguin, 1985)

Before analysing the passage above, I would like to explain briefly
why this book on *Reading Fiction* begins with Defoe's novel. Despite
the claims of several women writers such as Aphra Behn (especially
Oronooko, or the Royal Slave, 1688) and Mary de la Rivière Manley (for
example, *The Adventures of Rivella*, 1714), one of the most widely cited
critical works on eighteenth-century fiction asserts that: 'Robinson
Crusoe is certainly the first novel in the sense that it is the first fictional narrative in which an ordinary person's daily activities are the
centre of continuous literary attention.' (Watt, 1965: 74) Accordingly,
The Life and Strange Surprizing Adventures of Robinson Crusoe is a suitable text with which to begin this study of openings because it may
be seen as the first *realist* novel, and its beginning is a useful example
of the features of the genre. It is evident that Defoe is first of all
determined to persuade the reader of the actual existence of Crusoe.
Defoe's name does not appear on the 1719 title-page, and a Preface
places him in the position of editor to Crusoe's author. This 'editor'
writes that he 'believes the thing to be a just history of fact; neither is

there any appearance of fiction in it', a remarkable claim with which to introduce the 'first novel', but one which indicates a main principle of 'realism': verisimilitude, or truth to life.

So, turning to the opening paragraphs of the novel itself, we find that it begins with Crusoe telling us the most basic details that we would expect to read about someone from their autobiography: the place and year of their birth, the identity of their parents, their name and family origins. Defoe's first step in writing the novel is to try to convince the reader of the solid reality of 'Robinson Crusoe'. In other words, Defoe wishes the reader to believe that this is a 'real' or 'true' story and the attempt will be all the more convincing for being written in Crusoe's own voice. In brief, Defoe attempts what the French critic Roland Barthes has called 'the reality effect': the objective creation through innumerable believable details of a fictional world which is not a literal but an entirely plausible imitation of reality in which everything that happens, given an initial set of circumstances, appears logical and indeed likely. *Robinson Crusoe* is a good example because it is in part based on the adventures of a castaway Scot called Alexander Selkirk (1676–1721) but it aims to give the reader more than a historical account; Defoe wishes to provide an interesting narrative not of what actually *did* happen to a man marooned on an exotic island, but of what the reader is likely to believe *would* happen. In this way, Defoe and the many other early novelists who subtitled their books with such claims as 'A True History' (*Oronooko*) or 'The History of a Foundling'(Henry Fielding's *Tom Jones*, 1749) might distance themselves from the 'fancy' of the medieval romance and hope their imaginative fictions might outsell the major rivals for their readers' attention: history books. To add to this reality effect, Defoe also includes references to famous people, such as Sir William Lockhart (l.12), who did indeed lead the fight against the Spanish at Dunkirk in 1658.

According to many critics, the novel arose as a genre in England to correspond to the experiences of the emerging middle classes. The emphasis on mercantilism and commercial interests in *Robinson Crusoe* is thus explicable in terms of its catering for the interests of the bourgeoisie, who would be the novel's principal readers. Crusoe's efforts at methodical book-keeping embody European economic principles for several commentators, including Karl Marx, who, in Chapter 1 of his masterpiece, *Capital*, says that Crusoe's relations with the objects around him 'contain all that is essential to the determination of value': 'His stock-book contains a list of the objects of utility that belong to him, of the operations necessary for their production; and lastly, of the labour-time that definite quantities of those objects have, on an average, cost him.' For Marx, Crusoe is the archetypal bourgeois capitalist. There are however two other related aspects to Defoe's society that are crucial alongside an emphasis on the historical development of capitalism: individualism and Puritanism. The first places the individual's experience of the world at the centre of art as it does at the centre of economic and social responsibility. The second perceives human endeavour in terms of unremitting social and moral striving. Each individual is in the position of Robinson Crusoe, except that for most people life is exponentially complicated by the presence of others: for Crusoe, life is stripped to its essential struggle for warmth, shelter, food and territory. The question of companionship, interestingly, is resolved only by the introduction of a male slave, not a woman, because sex interferes with logic and industry, or a friend, because Crusoe must remain lord and master of his island.

Thus *Robinson Crusoe* is the story of an ordinary man, a younger son, from an industrious, reasonably prosperous family in the middle classes. The majority of the story will be concerned, however, with his isolation from family and society: with his personal rise from shipwrecked mariner to monarch of all he surveys. The narrative will be told in painstaking detail, as though it were a guidebook, with every character, place and event rendered fully present to the reader's mind through the narrator's personal testimony of his own unique experience. This is in line with the major philosophical texts of the time, which, though their ultimate aim was still to prove God's existence, took their cue from the French philosopher René Descartes' (1596–1650) *Discourse on Method*, with its central unshakeable proposition, *cogito ergo sum*: 'I think therefore I am.' Descartes is often thought of as having inaugurated modern philosophy, and the realist novel reflects his inquiries by concerning itself with detail, deduction, logic, and principles of cause and effect. Just as for Descartes the existence of God was to be proved by human reason, for novelists such as Defoe reality was to be explained in natural, empirical and rational (but not supernatural) terms.

The book opens with Defoe's narrator explaining who he is in a disarmingly ingenuous fashion. The most common beginning of an autobiography, and indeed the most common answer to the request 'Tell me about your life' would probably be 'I was born ...'. The reader learns several things about Crusoe from the first sentence, but it is noticeable that by the end of that sentence he has already shifted to talking about his family. After the opening line of the book the rest of the initial paragraph concerns his parents. The second paragraph also begins with Crusoe ('I'), but only as a means to identify his elder brothers, who are summarily dismissed as respectively dead and missing. It is therefore only in the third paragraph that the narrative moves to Crusoe himself, after having identified his parents and his siblings. This third paragraph, about the third son (l.16), therefore shifts to the key element of the novel in terms of both character and plot: Crusoe has a 'fatal' (l.24) attraction to the sea and this 'inclination' (l.21) will lead 'directly to [a] life of misery' (l.25) (see the discussion of prolepsis in the Introduction). Each of these paragraphs has followed the same structure: each begins with a statement about Crusoe ('I was ...', 'I had ...', 'Being the third son ...'), each is two sentences long, and each ends with the same word, 'me'. In other words, each of these paragraphs moves from Robinson as the subject of his narrative ('I') to Robinson as the object of his narrative ('me'). The opening therefore in some ways denies the centrality of Robinson to his own narrative, and also creates his identity in terms of others: even his name is not his own, but, on the one hand simply a combination of his parents' family names (his mother's family is 'Robinson', his father's 'Kreutznaer'), and on the other an Anglicised corruption of their surname: not 'Kreutznaer' but 'Crusoe'. This reflects a transition from 'I' ('I was called Robinson Kreutznaer': ll.6–7) to 'me' ('but by the usual corruption of words in England, we are now called, nay, we call our selves and write our name, Crusoe': ll.7–9). It is also an important narrative parallel that the colonialist autobiography of a European mastering a desert island begins after his father, 'being a foreigner' (l.2), has 'settled' (l.3) in the British Isles: a miniature version of the main story of the novel.

The third paragraph also ends with the 'bait' which should ensure that the reader continues the novel: 'the life of misery which was to befal me' (ll.25–6). It is a sentence which builds on the teasing sentence that ended the previous paragraph: 'What became of my second brother I never knew any more than my father or mother did know what was become of me' (ll.13–15). The key element of suspense is thus introduced on the first page to whet the reader's appetite.

The final paragraph adds to the reader's desire to know 'what became' of Crusoe by working on two levels: first, Crusoe explains that 'adventures' (l.37) should not have happened to him (at least according to his father) since he came from the 'middle state' (l.40) of life, and so the reader is further encouraged to wonder how a 'life of misery' (l.25) ensued; second, Crusoe, hailing from the middle classes, is established as someone with 'neither poverty or riches' (l.53), like most readers, and this adds to the vicarious pleasure that the reader can take in the events of the novel by imagining that similar adventures could 'befal' him or her.

This fourth paragraph, according to Lennard Davis, is the first 'scene' of the novel: one in which Crusoe is counselled by his father to be a good middle-class child (Davis, 1987: 60). It is the first 'scene' because the reader is provided with a setting: 'He called me one morning into his chamber' (l.29). Yet, the setting is general, as the time is, and serves simply as a backdrop, not as a particular location which the narrator makes any attempt to describe. For this reason, Davis argues that the novel begins in the style of the ballad, with a generalised sense of setting, and then moves to a specific, novelistic, use of location in the fully realised descriptions of the island. It is here that the novel, in its efforts to convince the reader of its authenticity, reaches towards the form of realism that prose fiction would evolve into over the next 200 years. This is an aspect to *Robinson Crusoe* that J. M. Coetzee emphasises in his 1986 re-working of Defoe's novel, *Foe*, in which a woman, Susan Barton, also marooned on the island, explains to Cruso(e):

> The truth that makes your story yours alone, that sets you apart from the old mariner by the fireside spinning yarns of sea-monsters and mermaids, resides in a thousand touches which today may seem of no importance, such as: When you made your needle (the needle you store in your belt), by what means did you pierce the eye? When you sewed your hat, what did you use for thread? Touches like these will one day persuade your countrymen that it is all true, every word, there was indeed once an island in the middle of the ocean where the wind blew and the gulls cried from the cliffs and a man named Cruso paced about in his apeskin clothes, scanning the horizon for a sail. (Penguin ed., p.18)

To achieve this ability to convince, the prose of *Robinson Crusoe* is formal and detailed, such that even the 12-line sentence beginning on line 35 is half the length of several sentences in the first few pages. The novel's style, which is sincere, inclusive and ponderous, echoes the judicious gravity of the narrator and his subject. Its objectivity and 'balanced' opinions also mirror the championing of balance and the middle way in Crusoe's father's speech. Above all, the language is referential. The use of imagination is never foregrounded, despite *Robinson Crusoe* being a fictional work, and the general air of objectivity in the novel suggests that fantasy is frivolous (and the origin of the story is of course not fantasy but the life of a contemporary). This is the perspective of Crusoe's father, who dislikes pride, luxury and ambition (l.45) as much as miseries and hardships (l.43). The paragraph ends with an allusion to the Book of Proverbs in the Bible: 'give me neither poverty nor riches' (30:8), and this is entirely in keeping with the sober sentiments expressed by Crusoe's father, who is himself an embodiment of the Protestant work ethic, as his son will come to be through the experience of being stranded on a remote island.

The last paragraph of this opening is a homage to the middle classes and to their achievements. It is they who lie behind this novel, as they do behind the novel genre; and it is also their achievements which inform the other major lens through which *Robinson Crusoe* can be read: colonialism. The most famous sections of the story concern Crusoe's conquering of an island, taming its wilderness, securing its resources and standing firm against its dangers, whether from nature or natives. It is therefore worth noting that the rise of the novel accompanied not only the rise of capitalism but also the spread of European colonialism. His father urges Robinson to stay, unlike himself, in his 'native country' (l.32), and 'raise his fortune by application and industry' (l.34). This is the philosophy of the merchant capitalist. But Crusoe wishes to seek his fortune outside his native country, as his father did, and become an adventurer. And while on first opening the text it seems to be about 'the strange surprizing adventures' of a shipwrecked sailor, its wider message appears to be that the rewards of both domestic capitalism and foreign colonialism, like the writing of a novel itself, will be secured through bourgeois individualism and the Protestant work ethic (see Childs, 1999).

Further Reading

Barthes, Roland (1970) *S/Z*, Oxford: Blackwell.
Childs, Peter (ed.) (1999) *Post-Colonial Theory and English Literature*, Edinburgh: Edinburgh University Press.
Davis, Lennard J. (1987) *Resisting Novels: Ideology and Fiction*, London: Methuen.
Day, Geoffrey (1987) *From Fiction to the Novel*, London: Routledge.
Watt, Ian (1965) *The Rise of the Novel*, Berkeley: University of California Press.

Laurence Sterne
The Life and Opinions of Tristram Shandy
(1759–67)

I wish either my father or my mother, or indeed both of them,
as they were in duty both equally bound to it, had minded what
they were about when they begot me; had they duly consider'd
how much depended upon what they were then doing;—that
not only the production of a rational Being was concern'd in it,   5
but that possibly the happy formation and temperature of his
body, perhaps his genius and the very cast of his mind;—and,
for aught they knew to the contrary, even the fortunes of his
whole house might take their turn from the humours and
dispositions which were then uppermost:—Had they duly   10
weighed and considered all this, and proceeded accordingly,
—I am verily persuaded I should have made a quite different
figure in the world, from that, in which the reader is likely to see
me.—Believe me, good folks, this is not so inconsiderable a
thing as many of you may think it;—you have all, I dare say,   15
heard of the animal spirits, as how they are transfused from
father to son, &c. &c.—and a great deal to that purpose:—Well,
you may take my word, that nine parts in ten of a man's sense or
his nonsense, his successes and miscarriages in this world depend upon their motions and activity, and the different tracks   20
and trains you put them into; so that when they are once set
a-going, whether right or wrong, 'tis not a halfpenny
matter,—away they go cluttering like hey-go-mad; and by
treading the same steps over and over again, they presently
make a road of it, as plain and as smooth as a garden-walk,   25
which, when they are once used to, the Devil himself sometimes
shall not be able to drive them off it.

   Pray, my dear, quoth my mother, *have you not forgot to wind
up the clock?—Good G–!* cried my father, making an exclamation, but taking care to moderate his voice at the same   30
time,—*Did ever woman, since the creation of the world,*

interrupt a man with such a silly question? Pray, what was your
father saying?—Nothing.

(Oxford: Oxford University Press, 1983)

This information concerning his conception is told to Tristram
Shandy by his Uncle Toby. Indeed, critics have remarked that the 'life
and opinions' of the book's title are in many ways not Tristram's
own, but based on his Uncle Toby's life and on his father's opinions.
In terms of content, the opening, we later find out, deals with the
moment Tristram was conceived, at an instant when his mother suddenly asked her husband if he had wound the clock, which he always
did on the same night each month when they had sex. In terms of
form, the opening poses clearly for the reader the question of when a
life begins, which is as complicated as the question of when a book
begins. Sterne is also concerned here, if very playfully, with the philosophical problem of when a human being becomes a human being: at
conception, at birth, at first consciousness or, even, at maturity? To
start an autobiography at 'the start' is to begin where? Similarly, the
same question is posed by a recent memoir, Blake Morrison's *And
When Did You Last See Your Father?* (1993), from the other end of a
lifespan. Morrison is not sure whether he should think the last time
he saw his father was when he saw his father's corpse, or saw him
before he died, or before he became ill with cancer, or when his father
last seemed 'completely himself': fully the man Morrison had known.
Tristram Shandy will actually take over a hundred pages to get
himself born, so punctilious is he in starting from the beginning of his
life: comically raising the problem of cause and effect, in life, in narrative, and in logic. Perhaps, in order to understand anything at all, we
need to know its circumstances and what preceded it, and in order
properly to understand those circumstances we need to know their
circumstances and what preceded them, and so on. Similarly, in order
to understand who Tristram Shandy is, perhaps we need to know
about his parents, and their parents, and so on, stretching back to
lives and circumstances far beyond the knowledge of anyone living.
It is best to stop this discussion here as otherwise, like many critics of
Sterne's novel, I will soon be repeating the digressive style of the
novel, which itself makes the point well that endless circumlocution
is inevitable as soon as one attempts, foolishly, to explain anything
fully, or perhaps even adequately. At such a pace, as many critics
have noted of *Tristram Shandy*, the narration of a life proceeds more
slowly than the life itself.

The 33 lines reprinted here comprise the first chapter of the novel. *Tristram Shandy* *appears* therefore to take his task very seriously, and in recounting his life begins with his conception, an event at which, like his own death, he might be said both to have been present and to have not been. One of the cues for this beginning is the Roman poet Horace's distinction, alluded to in chapter 4 of the novel, between stories that start *ab ovo*, and those, which Horace actually preferred, that commence *in media res*: between stories that begin at the beginning, or 'from the egg', like life, and those which begin in the middle. Yet, from other perspectives, Tristram does begin in the middle of things; first, in the sense of starting with a *coitus interruptus*, or more properly a man distracted at the moment of ejaculation, and second, because this opening tells the reader hardly anything about the characters or their circumstances. As an opening, though it starts with its subject, 'I' (l.1), the first word, what it tells the reader about that subject is precisely 'Nothing' (l.33), the final word. The opening therefore appears not to start at 'the beginning', certainly not in the way in which *Robinson Crusoe* did ('I was born in the year 1632 ...'), but 'in the middle', in the sense that it begins nowhere: the start is no 'start' at all, in terms of autobiography; it is only a start in terms of the text. Metaphorically speaking, Tristram has forgotten to wind up the clock of his autobiography and so the narration of his life is not progressing just as an unwound clock will not progress in time: will stop. Perhaps the only thing that is being 'wound up' is the reader.

Tristram Shandy therefore starts with a false start, in terms of its being a narrative of Tristram's life; and the rest of the book will proceed via, if not as, a series of interruptions. It is also an interruption in terms of what it narrates: Tristram's mother interrupts his father by suddenly asking in the middle of coitus '*Pray, my dear, ... have you not forgot to wind up the clock?*'. The interruption is of course both an ejaculation (hers) and the interruption of an ejaculation (his). An eighteenth-century audience would also not need Freud to explain the sexual symbolism of winding up a clock, and similarly readers would be expected to note the significance of the final speech: *Did ever woman, since the creation of the world, interrupt a man with such a silly question?* The mention of the world's creation at the moment of describing Tristram's creation is perhaps mere rhetoric, or just a sign of Tristram's sense of self-importance, but it is also an allusion by Sterne to Eve's temptation of Adam (the Edenic parallels are also there in the 'garden-walk' (l.25) and the reference to people's natures [original sin and 'treading the same steps over and over again' (ll.23–4)] which 'the Devil himself sometimes shall not be able to drive them off': 1.26). It was of course Adam and Eve's not having properly 'minded what they were about' (ll.2–3), as 'they were in duty both equally bound to'(l.2), which led to the fall of 'man', just as Tristram in this first chapter is concerned with his parent's part in his own fall from greatness: 'Had they duly weighed and considered all this, and proceeded accordingly—I am verily persuaded I should have made a quite different figure in the world.' (ll.10–13). The reason for this 'fall' is that in the eighteenth century it was believed that the 'quality' of a man's ejaculation determined the quality of the child produced from it. His father's distraction has therefore been the 'seed' of Tristram's shortcomings, so to speak. Tristram is thus laying at his parents' door all his own failings; most particularly because of the medieval belief that the body's four chief fluids or cardinal 'humours' (l.9), blood, phlegm, choler and melancholy, transmitted by the sperm, determined an individual's physical and mental qualities (this is discussed at greater length in Tristram's second chapter).

There are many words in the passage that relate to the act Tristram's parents are engaged in, such as 'formation' (l.6), 'cast' (l.7), 'miscarriages' (l.19) and 'motions' (l.20). Even the very style, its rhythm and turns, might be considered a representation of the sexual act, though of course the long, digressive sentences and complex syntax are features of eighteenth-century prose which would today be considered convoluted and overly formal. It is also a style well suited to describing a delicate subject in a roundabout manner. The style is additionally capacious, almost all-encompassing. Sterne attempts to fit everything into the sentence before he finishes it, and this is an example of the way in which each sentence is a microcosm of Tristram's whole project. It is a recognisably eighteenth-century endeavour, to write a book that contains every last detail: to contain the world, or at least one person's world, in one book. In this respect *Tristram Shandy* would sit comfortably on the bookshelf alongside other monumental works of the Enlightenment: Dr Johnson's *Dictionary of the English Language* (1755), David Hume's five-volume *History of England* (1754–62), or the first Chambers' *Cyclopedia* (1728), from which Sterne playfully took various ideas on myriad subjects.

To begin the novel with a conception also seems appropriate, arguably drawing parallels with the way in which Tristram's parents should have 'minded what they were about' (ll.2–3) and the way in which a novelist creates both a book and, in the figure of the hero, a 'Rational Being' or character. It is a critical commonplace to say that *Tristram Shandy* was published centuries before its time. It appears as postmodern, as self-referential and experimental, as a book published 200 years later. This is not just the view from the present; a contemporary reviewer in the *Royal Female Magazine* declared that Sterne's novel 'affects (and not unsuccessfully) to please, by a contempt for all the rules observed in other writings, and therefore cannot justly have its merit measured by them'. Yet it is also important to remember that Sterne is writing at a time when self-referentiality was common (consider the openings to Jonathan Swift's *A Tale of a Tub*, 1704, or Alexander Pope's *The Dunciad*, 1728), and also that the opening of the novel does not in any way 'break its frame' and refer to itself as a novel, or the work of not Tristram Shandy but Laurence Sterne.

However, the novel's title page carries a quotation from the ancient Greek philosopher Epictetus: 'Human beings are harried not by things, but by opinions about things.' Tristram is indeed worried about opinions: his own, of course, his father's, and especially, to shift the emphasis of the word's meaning from 'view and judgment' to 'evaluation or impression', the opinion of the world. Here again Sterne is concerned with a philosophical debate current in the seventeenth and eighteenth centuries: do we perceive physical objects, or only 'ideas' and 'impressions'? The major intertext here is the empiricist John Locke's *Essay Concerning Human Understanding* (1690) which maintains that everything the mind contains comes from experience, and that there are no innate ideas or principles. The individual is born with a mind as blank as a new sheet of paper: which provides one way for Tristram to think of (and perhaps delimit) the origin of his life and even his opinions.

Further Reading

New, Melvyn (ed.) (1992) *The Life and Opinions of Tristram Shandy, Gentleman* London: Macmillan – now Palgrave.

Richetti, John (1998) *The English Novel in History: 1700–1780*, London: Routledge.

Traugott, John (ed.) (1968) *Laurence Sterne: A Collection of Critical Essays.* Englewood Cliffs, NJ: Prentice-Hall.

Jane Austen
Pride and Prejudice
(1813)

It is a truth universally acknowledged, that a single man in
possession of a good fortune, must be in want of a wife.

However little known the feelings or views of such a man may
be on his first entering a neighbourhood, this truth is so well fixed
in the minds of the surrounding families, that he is considered as   5
the rightful property of some one or other of their daughters.

'My dear Mr Bennet,' said his lady to him one day, 'have you
heard that Netherfield Park is let at last?'

Mr Bennet replied that he had not.

'But it is,' returned she; 'for Mrs Long has just been here, and   10
she told me all about it.'

Mr Bennet made no answer.

'Do not you want to know who has taken it?' cried his wife
impatiently.

'*You* want to tell me, and I have no objection to hearing it.'   15

This was invitation enough.

'Why, my dear, you must know, Mrs Long says that Netherfield is taken by a young man of large fortune from the north of
England; that he came down on Monday in a chaise and four to
see the place, and was so much delighted with it that he agreed   20
with Mr Morris immediately; that he is to take possession before
Michelmas, and some of his servants are to be in the house by
the end of next week.'

'What is his name?'

'Bingley.'   25

'Is he married or single?'

'Oh! Single, my dear, to be sure! A single man of large fortune;
four or five thousand a year. What a fine thing for our girls!'

'How so? how can it affect them?'

'My dear Mr Bennet,' replied his wife, 'how can you be so   30
tiresome! You must know that I am thinking of his marrying one

of them.'

   'Is that his design in settling here?'

   'Design! nonsense, how can you talk so! But it is very likely
that he *may* fall in love with one of them, and therefore you must   35
visit him as soon as he comes.'

   'I see no occasion for that. You and the girls may go, or you
may send them by themselves, which perhaps will be still better,
for as you are as handsome as any of them, Mr Bingley might like
you the best of the party.'   40

   'My dear, you flatter me. I certainly *have* had my share of
beauty, but I do not pretend to be any thing extraordinary now.
When a woman has five grown up daughters, she ought to give
over thinking of her own beauty.'

   'In such cases, a woman has not often much beauty to think of.'   45

   'But, my dear, you must indeed go and see Mr Bingley when he
comes into the neighbourhood.'

   'It is more than I engage for, I assure you.'

   'But consider your daughters. Only think what an establishment it would be for one of them. Sir William and Lady Lucas   50
are determined to go, merely on that account, for in general you
know they visit no new comers. Indeed you must go, for it will
be impossible for *us* to visit him, if you do not.'

   'You are over scrupulous surely. I dare say Mr Bingley will be
very glad to see you; and I will send a few lines by you to assure   55
him of my hearty consent to his marrying which ever he chuses
of the girls; though I must throw in a good word for my little
Lizzy.'

                                   (Harmondsworth: Penguin, 1972)

The opening chapter of Austen's novel, as with several of her others,
establishes the story that will unfold over the hundreds of pages that
follow. Aside from the opening 16 lines, and the closing paragraph,
the approximately 85-line chapter is composed almost entirely of
untagged dialogue, with only two reporting clauses: 'replied his
wife' (l.30), and then later 'replied he'. In other words, with few
exceptions the characters speak directly to the reader throughout. As
there is so little description (we know almost nothing about this
couple with regard to their physical appearance or surroundings),
the chapter is perhaps most concerned with the revelation of character: by its close the reader has a firm grasp of Mr and Mrs Bennet's
personalities and of their relationship. Austen does this not through

diegesis, allowing the narrator to explain to the reader, but through *mimesis,* the direct speech of the characters. Which is to say, the reader is shown the characters and their dialogue, not told about them. Austen's technique is essentially realist: like Defoe she aims to offer up a mirror to the world, but hers is a markedly different world from that of *Robinson Crusoe. Pride and Prejudice* features characters, language, and a spatial and temporal setting familiar to its bourgeois readers. As with most other realist novels, the time is the contemporary, the place ordinary, the people from the middle classes, the ideology secular, the language everyday, and the narrator above the characters in a 'hierarchy of discourse' that allows the third-person narrator to be unquestionable as well as omniscient. Most importantly, *Pride and Prejudice* presents itself as transparently representative of the author's society, and of the society of its contemporary readers (for example, contrast this with Shakespearean tragedy which uses poetry, the nobility and locations usually distant in time and place).

In his introduction to the Everyman edition of *Tristram Shandy,* George Saintsbury notes about Sterne's marriage that 'It has been a steady rule in the Anglican Church ... that when a man has been provided with a living, he should, if he has not done so before, provide himself with a wife.' As though Jane Austen were transferring this rule to the secular world as a 'truth', *Pride and Prejudice* begins with one of her most famous uses of irony. The first sentence takes a local attitude, to be exemplified in Mrs Bennet, about the need of well-to-do men to marry, and transforms it, tongue-in-cheek, into a self-evident fact 'universally acknowledged'. The second paragraph reveals the provenance of this 'truth' to be the genteel families of a 'neighbourhood', as yet unspecified. The community's interest in wealth is made clear in the narrator's expression that the young man 'in possession' of money must be 'the rightful property' of one of their young women. A society based on ownership and money, marriage and 'fortune', is thus established. There are clearly rules to be observed, which is why Mrs Bennet is so anxious for her husband to initiate an acquaintance with Mr Bingley. There is mention of love, but only in relation to Bingley; Mrs Bennet appears unconcerned with whether her daughters might love him. Perhaps most startlingly to a modern reader, Mrs Bennet hears wedding bells for one of her daughters, and she is indifferent to which one, as soon as she is aware of a new eligible bachelor in the community, even though she denies having 'designs' (1.34) on Bingley. By the way in which the characters are presented (her exclamations and his cool-headed-ness) the reader is immediately encouraged to side with Mr Bennet, but the fervour with which Mrs Bennet contemplates the (seemingly distant) possibility of one of her daughters wedding Mr Bingley indicates the social and economic importance to a family with five daughters both to relieve themselves of the financial burden of a young woman who is unlikely to bring them in much if any money, and to acquire influence and status through a prestigious marriage. It is also important to remember, if the reader is tempted to laugh at Mrs Bennet, that her eldest daughter does indeed end the novel married to Mr Bingley. Which is to say that the novel's beginning foresees its end, indicating the tight organisation of the novel and its circular structure, and also that Mrs Bennet's encouragement of her husband to visit Mr Bingley, which he does, makes her the principal matchmaker in a novel that is fundamentally about the importance of making a 'good' marriage, whether defined by personal compatibility or social standing. The final chapter, set a little over a year later, begins with: 'Happy for all her maternal feelings was the day on which Mrs Bennet got rid of her two most deserving daughters', a sentence with almost as much irony as the far more famous opening line of the novel. A point to note here is that the Bennets do not have a son to succeed them and, according to the law of their time, their daughters cannot inherit their estate. The narrative twists and turns of the novel are thus precipitated by the arrival of a series of eligible men into the estates around the village of Longbourn. In this, the novel follows a clear and common narrative trajectory from stability (social and familial) through a number of potential and actual changes to a new state of equilibrium at the end.

After the opening paragraph, the rhythm of the chapter is created by two exchanges between Mr and Mrs Bennet, followed by his capitulation to her: '*You* want to tell me, and I have no objection to hearing it' (1.15). Her insistent garrulous nature and his reticence to speak unnecessarily are immediately suggested by the fact that her speech is reported directly whereas his reactions are indirectly and perfunctorily described by the narrator: 'Mr Bennet replied that he had not' (1.9) and 'Mr Bennet made no answer' (1.12). The similar construction suggests the frequency of such conversations between the married couple and also Mr Bennet's patient, if teasing and 'tiresome' (1.31), indulgence of his impatient (1.14) wife. Their relationship is underlined by the fact that he is repeatedly referred to by the narrator as 'Mr Bennet', while she is variously 'his lady' (1.7) and 'his wife' (1.13): a practice which imitates the characters' own habits (Mrs Bennet uses her husband's name, but he does not use hers). Mrs

Bennet, a name-dropper, uses her husband's name the better to secure his attention; Mr Bennet does not use his wife's name because he does not wish to engage in the conversation at all.

The statement of his lack of curiosity is 'invitation enough' (1.16) for his wife to communicate her excitement, and build up to her request, despite his indifference. Mrs Bennet's next speech, the longest of the chapter, and beginning with the gossipy 'Why, my dear, you must know ...' (1.17), now initiates a series of four questions and answers. Mr Bennet finally agrees to play ball, and when it is soon discovered that Bingley is a 'single man of large fortune', Mr and Mrs Bennet adopt the positions outlined in the chapter's opening two paragraphs: Mrs Bennet concludes that it is 'a fine thing for our girls' (1.28) because Bingley will want to take a wife, while Mr Bennet ponders the 'feelings or views of such a man ... first entering a neighbourhood' (ll.3–4) when he disingenuously asks: 'Is that his design in settling here?' (1.33).

The rest of the extract centres on Mr Bennet's teasing of his wife: if Mr Bingley wants a wife perhaps he will want Mr Bennet's (ll.39–40); Mr Bennet does not seek to 'engage' (1.48) Mr Bingley even if his wife wishes to engage one of her daughters to him; if Mrs Bennet is so sure she wishes to marry one of her daughters to Mr Bingley without ever having seen the man, Mr Bennet is similarly happy to give his consent without going to visit him (ll.55–6).

Since Mr Bennet will not attend seriously to his wife's main interest – 'I am thinking of [Bingley] marrying one of [our girls]' (1.31) – and does not share the 'universal' view of the chapter's opening sentence, Mrs Bennet is reduced to the occasional 'Oh' (1.27), and later in the chapter 'Ah!', and other exclamations. The closing paragraph of the chapter summarises their two positions, just as the opening paragraphs introduced them: 'Mr Bennet was so odd a mixture of quick parts, sarcastic humour, reserve, and caprice, that the experience of three and twenty years had been insufficient to make his wife understand his character ... The business of her life was to get her daughters married; its solace was visiting and news.' The reader may be left wondering how Mr and Mrs Bennet ever became married themselves, and ask: of what fortune was Mr Bennet in possession?

Finally, the opening might be read, along with most of the novel, in terms of the characters' vanities and weaknesses, most particularly those of pride and prejudice. Elizabeth Bennet's key self-insight will occur when she realises that 'she had been blind, partial, prejudiced, absurd' when she had 'prided [herself] on [her] discernment' (p.236).

The novel is not didactic but aims to illustrate the ways in which stereotypes, based on our exaggerated sense of self-importance or self-worth, vitiate our impression of others, which would be more firmly based on observation and understanding. This sizeable gap between what we believe, and what greater knowledge, sympathy and reflection might persuade us to believe, forms the space that allows Austen's narrator consistently to adopt a tone of irony which, as discussed in the Introduction, is prevalent in so much fiction principally concerned with social interaction.

Further Reading

Butler, Marilyn (1987) *Jane Austen and the War of Ideas* (rev. edn), Oxford: Clarendon.
Spencer, J. (1986) *The Rise of the Woman Novelist: From Aphra Behn to Jane Austen*, Oxford: Basil Blackwell.
Walder, Dennis (ed.) (1995) *The Realist Novel*, London: Routledge.

Mary Shelley
Frankenstein
(1818)

To Mrs Saville, England
St Petersburgh, Dec. 11th 17—

You will rejoice to hear that no disaster has accompanied the
commencement of an enterprize which you have regarded with
such evil forebodings. I arrived here yesterday; and my first task is
to assure my dear sister of my welfare and increasing confidence in
the success of my undertaking.   5
   I am already far north of London; and as I walk in the streets of
Petersburgh, I feel a cold northern breeze play upon my cheeks,
which braces my nerves and fills me with delight. Do you understand this feeling? This breeze, which has travelled from the regions
towards which I am advancing, gives me a foretaste of those icy   10
climes. Inspirited by this wind of promise, my daydreams become
more fervent and vivid. I try in vain to be persuaded that the pole
is the seat of frost and desolation; it ever presents itself to my
imagination as the region of beauty and delight. There, Margaret,
the sun is forever visible, its broad disk just skirting the horizon   15
and diffusing a perpetual splendour. There — for with your leave,
my sister, I will put some trust in preceding navigators — there
snow and frost are banished; and, sailing over a calm sea, we may
be wafted to a land surpassing in wonders and in beauty every
region hitherto discovered on the habitable globe. Its productions   20
and features may be without example, as the phaenomena of the
heavenly bodies undoubtedly are in those undiscovered solitudes.
What may not be expected in a country of eternal light? I may
there discover the wondrous power which attracts the needle and
may regulate a thousand celestial observations that require only   25
this voyage to render their seeming eccentricities consistent forever. I shall satiate my ardent curiosity with the sight of a part of
the world never before visited, and may tread a land never before

imprinted by the foot of man. These are my enticements, and they
are sufficient to conquer all fear of danger or death and to induce   30
me to commence this laborious voyage with the joy a child feels
when he embarks in a little boat, with his holiday mates, on an
expedition of discovery up his native river. But supposing all these
conjectures to be false, you cannot contest the inestimable benefit
which I shall confer on all mankind to the last generation, by   35
discovering a passage near the pole to those countries, to reach
which at present so many months are requisite; or by ascertaining
the secret of the magnet, which, if at all possible, can only be
effected by an undertaking such as mine.

    These reflections have dispelled the agitation with which I began 40
my letter, and I feel my heart glow with an enthusiasm which
elevates me to heaven; for nothing contributes so much to tranquillize the mind as a steady purpose – a point on which the soul
may fix its intellectual eye. This expedition has been the favourite
dream of my early years. I have read with ardour the accounts of   45
the various voyages which have been made in the prospect of
arriving at the North Pacific Ocean through the seas which surround the pole. You may remember that a history of all the voyages
made for purposes of discovery composed the whole of our good
Uncle Thomas's library. My education was neglected, yet I was   50
passionately fond of reading. These volumes were my study day
and night, and my familiarity with them increased that regret
which I had felt, as a child, on learning that my father's dying
injunction had forbidden my uncle to allow me to embark in a
seafaring life.   55

                                (Harmondsworth: Penguin, 1985)

Mary Shelley's book opens with a frame narration which, as it is in
the form of a letter, recalls the earlier epistolary novels of Samuel
Richardson (for example, *Clarissa* (1747–8)) and others. Before the
book's main chapters begin, there are four letters written by the man
who records Victor Frankenstein's account of his life, Captain
Walton. These are addressed to Walton's sister, Margaret Saville. The
letters are sent by Walton as he travels nearer to the North Pole: the
first three before he even meets Frankenstein, and the fourth after.
The Swiss scientist Frankenstein has been led to the Arctic by the
'monster', the reader later learns, because his creation is 'impassive'
to the cold. From Shelley's point of view, the bleak Arctic represents
the same sublime (but treacherous) Romantic landscape as do the

Alps in poems such as her husband Percy Shelley's 'Mont Blanc' or Xanadu in Coleridge's 'Kubla Khan'. The frame is particularly interesting because it is written in a different form from the main narrative. Shelley chooses to use the epistolary convention of authors such as Richardson for this preface before the descriptive and digressive first-person account of Frankenstein takes over the novel. This technique itself seems to hand over the novel from one older style to another newer one, just as the narrative seems to switch between Gothic and realist conventions. After the rise of the realist novel to express the new world of mercantile capitalism and bourgeois individualism, epitomised in *Robinson Crusoe*, Gothic arose according to David Punter 'at the stage when the bourgeoisie, having to all intents and purposes gained social power, began to try to understand the conditions and history of their own ascent ... Gothic is thus a form of response to the emergence of a middle-class-dominated capitalist society'. Punter therefore positions Gothic as the flipside of realism, and the blend of the two in Shelley's novel can certainly be viewed in terms of many oppositions in the narrative, including that between Frankenstein and his 'monster'. Punter concludes that Gothic emerges because, with the

> coming of industry, the move towards the city, the regularisation of patterns of labour in the late eighteenth century ... the individual comes to see him- or herself at the mercy of forces which in fundamental ways elude understanding. Under such circumstances it is hardly surprising to find the emergence of a literature whose key motifs are paranoia, manipulation, and injustice, and whose central project is understanding the inexplicable, the taboo, the irrational. (Punter, 1996: 112)

Shelley's novel may thus be seen in terms of a conflict between social attitudes, styles, characters, and even narrators, as the story comes to the reader through both Frankenstein's and Walton's narration. As with other first-person frame accounts, Walton's is added here to attest to the veracity of the main story. We are expected to give Frankenstein's narrative more credence because it is told to us by someone who witnessed the telling of it (as with James's *The Turn of the Screw* or Conrad's *Heart of Darkness*). The frame narration also works in a complex way in relation to the rest of the novel. As we read on towards the middle of the book we find that we move from Walton's account to Frankenstein's and then down another level to the 'monster's' (it is worth noting that there are also embedded stories within this, such as Safie's in Chapter 14). This gives the reader the impression of moving closer to the centre of the story as

Walton travels nearer to the Pole. Walton's thoughts, as he is 'far north of London' (l.6) and travelling further northward, lead him, like Frankenstein, to contemplate an achievement which should not be hoped for by humans. Frankenstein seeks to gain power over life and death, which is God's prerogative, and Walton dreams of the Pole as God's realm: he wishes to reach a 'country of eternal light' (l.23) and he says that on this quest his 'heart glows with an enthusiasm which elevates me to heaven' (ll.41–2).

The opening to *Frankenstein* is one of those which superficially appears to bear no relation to the central story of the novel, and yet on closer inspection is entirely relevant to it, introducing and throwing light on many of the book's main themes. One way to consider the beginning's importance is in relation to the book's subtitle, *The Modern Prometheus*: a phrase which had been in use for a century before 1818 to refer to scientists who seemed dangerously to follow Prometheus's example by coveting forbidden knowledge (though the term 'scientist' itself did not in fact exist until 1840). Most famously, Prometheus is known for stealing fire, for humans, from the ancient Greek Gods; but he was also credited in some Greek mythology with the creation of human beings, and this is the most obvious connection between Prometheus and Frankenstein. The story we read, as told to Captain Walton by Victor Frankenstein, is expressly aimed at dissuading him from embarking on a course of exploration that may lead to his death. Frankenstein sees a parallel between their two endeavours and warns Walton, who is searching for the North Pole, that he underestimates the dangers which await those who sin against nature or God. Walton's sister, to whom he writes this letter, had similar fears and, we know, 'regarded' his voyage 'with such evil forebodings' (ll.2–3). Like Frankenstein, Walton will not be deterred from his task: 'I try in vain to be persuaded that the pole is the seat of frost and desolation' (ll.12–13). Instead, like the Swiss scientist, he believes egotistically that his goal is attainable and glorious: 'it ever presents itself to my imagination as the region of beauty and delight' (ll.13–4). On one level, then, the novel's message is clearly that overweening pride and selfish, solitary pursuits foster unforeseen evils, and should be rejected for generous and wholesome social relationships.

This first letter precedes Walton's encounter with Frankenstein but exhibits several parallels with the story that follows. Like Frankenstein, Walton feels 'increasing confidence in the success of my undertaking' (ll.4–5). The 'cold northern breeze' in St. Petersburgh, his penultimate stop in civilisation before venturing into the Arctic waste, only 'braces my nerves and fills me with delight' (l.8), such that 'Inspirited by this wind of promise, my day-dreams become more fervent and vivid' (ll. 11–12). Walton has the same familiar Romantic feeling that nature is benign and gently guiding as Wordsworth has at the beginning of *The Prelude*: 'Oh there is a blessing in this gentle breeze ...'. Walton's misguided idea of the Arctic is of an otherworldly paradise: 'there snow and frost are banished; and, sailing over a calm sea, we may be wafted to a land surpassing in wonders and in beauty every region hitherto discovered on the habitable globe' (ll.17–20). He sees it as an Edenic discovery: 'I shall satiate my ardent curiosity with the sight of a part of the world never before visited', and also as a territorial claim: 'and may tread a land never before imprinted by the foot of man' (ll. 28–9). These last words, overconscious of the personal glory involved in boldly going where no one has gone before, even seem to presage those famously used by Neil Armstrong when he walked on the moon in 1969 (indeed, lines 21–2 compare Walton's journey into the Arctic with that into 'undiscovered' space). Walton's words are, however, extreme, bordering on the monomaniacal. The pole he searches for is a myth, and so the search for it can only end in tragedy. Luckily for him, his sailors will refuse to risk their lives on this folly, and so save him from his 'imagination' (l.14), which he has tried 'in vain' (l.12) to turn away from. Frankenstein, by contrast, worked entirely alone, and without the benefit of other voices, of society, to correct his extreme egotism.

Walton's greatest hope, like Frankenstein's desire to gain the knowledge of how to reanimate dead tissue, is at the Pole to 'discover the wondrous power which attracts the needle' (l.24): 'the secret of the magnet' (l.38). It is these dreams that for Walton, as they did for Frankenstein, foolishly 'conquer all fear of danger and death' (l.30). In his vision of 'the inestimable benefit which I shall confer on mankind to the last generation' (ll.34–5), Walton replicates Prometheus's intention to give the gift of fire to humanity despite the dangers to them and the risk of punishment by the Gods to himself. The implied threat of punishment for Walton from the Christian God ('Our Father who art in Heaven') is clear at the end of this extract when the reader learns that: 'my father's dying injunction had forbidden my uncle to allow me to embark in a seafaring life' (ll.53–5). Both here (l.53) and earlier (l.31) Walton thinks of himself as 'a child', hinting at Shelley's concern with, first, humanity's defiance of the laws of God the Father (only God has the power to give life), and second, the rebellion that will be mounted against Frankenstein by his child/creation.

Walton, like Frankenstein, learns his dream from books (ll.45–52), and both he and Frankenstein fail to see that 'a steady purpose – a point on which the soul may fix its intellectual eye' (ll.43–4) can lead to misjudgement. Walton considers that his 'enthusiasm' and 'ardour' dispel his 'agitation' and 'tranquillize the mind', but the banishing of real fears and a numbness towards danger are themselves easy ways to ensure pain and suffering (ll.40–5).

The extract ends with a passage very similar to one we have already encountered, at the start of *Robinson Crusoe*. Crusoe says of his youth: 'I would be satisfied with nothing but going to sea, and my inclinations to this led me so strongly against all the will, nay, the commands of my father ... that there seemed to be something fatal in that propension of nature tending directly to the life of misery which was to befal me' (ll.20–6). The opening extract from Shelley ends with Walton remembering the 'regret which I had felt, as a child, on learning that my father's dying injunction had forbidden my uncle to allow me to embark on a seafaring life'. Both novels increase the reader's sense of adventure by drawing on childhood dreams and on romantic notions of life at sea. Both also strike a note of foreboding that the novels use for different effects: Defoe to prepare the reader for Crusoe's shipwreck; Shelley for Frankenstein's parallel story of adventure and Walton's decision to turn back.

Thus, from its opening page, a debate takes place in *Frankenstein* over, on the one hand, what it is to be in (self-)control, command or authority and, on the other, what it means to be 'human'. This is largely a question of moral responsibility towards others: the responsibility of the parent, of the scientist, and of the leader. It is a question of social accountability and of human contact. If we resist and at worst refuse human contact to others then we injure both them and ourselves. In this, the novel attacks as much as it depicts images of the solitary genius, the noble hermit, or the Romantic wanderer who seeks to gain at best inspiration, and at worst pre-eminence, from science or nature at the expense of humanity.

Further Reading

Baldick, Chris (1987) *In Frankenstein's Shadow: Myth, Monstrosity and Nineteenth-Century Writing*, Oxford: Clarendon.

Gilbert, Sandra and Gubar, Susan (1979) *The Madwoman in the Attic: The Woman Writer and the Nineteenth-Century Literary Imagination*, New Haven, CT: Yale University Press.

Moers, Ellen (1972) *Literary Women*, London: Women's Press.
Punter, David (1996) *The Literature of Terror*, Volume One: The Gothic
Tradition (2nd edn), Essex: Longman.

Charlotte Brontë
Jane Eyre
(1847)

There was no possibility of taking a walk that day. We had been
wandering, indeed, in the leafless shrubbery an hour in the morning;
but since dinner (Mrs Reed, when there was no company, dined early)
the cold winter wind had brought with it clouds so sombre, and a rain
so penetrating, that further out-door exercise was now out of the   5
question.

I was glad of it: I never liked long walks, especially on chilly
afternoons: dreadful to me was the coming home in the raw twilight,
with nipped fingers and toes, and a heart saddened by the chidings of
Bessie, the nurse, and humbled by the consciousness of my physical   10
inferiority to Eliza, John, and Georgiana Reed.

The said Eliza, John, and Georgiana were now clustered round
their mama in the drawing-room: she lay reclined on a sofa by the
fireside, and with her darlings about her (for the time neither quarrelling
nor crying) looked perfectly happy. Me, she had dispensed from joining 15
the group; saying, 'She regretted to be under the necessity of keeping
me at a distance; but that until she heard from Bessie, and could
discover by her own observation that I was endeavouring in good
earnest to acquire a more sociable and child-like disposition, a more
attractive and sprightly manner – something lighter, franker, more   20
natural as it were – she really must exclude me from privileges intended
only for contented, happy, little children.'

'What does Bessie say I have done?' I asked.

'Jane, I don't like cavillers or questioners: besides, there is
something truly forbidding in a child taking up her elders in that   25
manner. Be seated somewhere; and until you can speak pleasantly,
remain silent.'

A small breakfast-room adjoined the drawing-room. I slipped
in there. It contained a book-case: I soon possessed myself of a
volume, taking care that it should be one stored with pictures. I   30
mounted into the window-seat: gathering up my feet, I sat cross-

legged, like a Turk; and, having drawn the red moreen curtain
nearly close, I was shrined in double retirement.
   Folds of scarlet drapery shut in my view to the right hand;
to the left were the clear panes of glass, protecting, but not   35
separating me from the drear November day. At intervals, while
turning over the leaves of my book, I studied the aspect of that
winter afternoon. Afar, it offered a pale blank of mist and cloud;
near, a scene of wet lawn and storm-beat shrub, with ceaseless rain
sweeping away wildly before a long and lamentable blast.   40
   I returned to my book – Bewick's History of British Birds: the
letter-press thereof I cared little for, generally speaking; and yet there
were certain introductory pages that, child as I was, I could not pass
quite as a blank. They were those which treat of the haunts of sea-fowl;
of 'the solitary rocks and promontories' by them only inhabited; of the   45
coast of Norway, studded with isles from its southern extremity, the
Lindeness, or Naze, to the North Cape.

(Harmondsworth: Penguin, 1966)

Like *Great Expectations* and *A Portrait of the Artist as a Young Man, Jane Eyre* can be called a *Bildungsroman*. This German term denotes a kind of autobiographical fiction that came to the fore in the late eighteenth century – the seminal example is Goethe's *Wilhelm Meister's Apprenticeship* (1796) – concerned with an individual's education. Such novels are stories of growing up, maturation and social development, most often in the first person, and usually confessional in tone. In *Jane Eyre*, the form of the narrative is the common one in *Bildungsromans* of a reflection on personal growth from childhood through to adolescence and beyond, told with the experience of adulthood. Jane will thus reveal not just 'her story', but the events that have made the child at the start of the book into the adult who addresses the reader.

   The most striking aspect of this opening is the way in which inner and outer worlds parallel each other: nature is in harmony with Jane's condition as though parallel human emotions were ascribed to the elements (see the glossary entry on personification, and also on pathetic fallacy, a term coined only a few years after the publication of *Jane Eyre*). However, this is not always the case in the novel, and the most famous example of Brontë's deployment of nature to comment upon the human world is an incident whose significance is lost on Jane at the time, but ominously recollected by her older self. It occurs when Jane and Rochester have agreed to marry, even though Rochester knows he is still married to Bertha Mason, and the extreme weather acts like a Greek chorus to warn her:

> joy soon effaced every other feeling; and loud as the wind blew, near and deep as the thunder crashed, fierce and frequent as the lightning gleamed, cataract-like as the rain fell during a storm of two hours' duration, I experienced no fear, and little awe ... Before I left my bed in the morning, little Adèle came running in to tell me that the great horse-chestnut at the bottom of the orchard had been struck by lightning in the night, and half of it split away. (End of Chapter 23)

In these first paragraphs, by contrast, the bleak November day is employed by Brontë to reflect Jane's mood and the misery of her life is matched by the bitter weather. In the penultimate paragraph, excluded from Mrs Reed's family circle, she describes herself 'in double retirement' between drapery which 'shut in my view to the right hand' and only a window 'protecting, but not separating me from the drear November day' to the left (ll.35–6). Also, it is worth considering Brontë's use of language to create particular effects: for example, there is the alliterative 'w' and 'l' sounds arranged to create a sense of mournful loneliness in the description of the rain on the 'wet lawn': 'sweeping away wildly before a long and lamentable blast' (ll.39–40) (see the glossary entries on alliteration and assonance).

The opening sentence is curiously ominous. Its negative stress appears to fall on everything. The narrator emphasises that there will be *no* walk that afternoon without confining her comment to herself or to any other people: there is simply 'no possibility', as though the impossibility were total. The bleakness of the day is then repeatedly stated and implied: 'cold winter wind', 'clouds so sombre', 'rain so penetrating' (ll.4–5). All of these echo the terms used to describe Jane's feelings: 'dreadful to me', 'a heart saddened', 'humbled by ... my physical inferiority' (ll.8–11). Jane's harsh treatment by Mrs Reed appears to be repeated in the way in which nature gives her 'nipped fingers and toes' (l.9).

Brontë's style may best be seen from the second paragraph, which consists of one long sentence. It is a paragraph sitting between two others which are composed of two sentences: one comparatively short followed by one very long. The second paragraph's one long sentence is broken into clauses by commas, but also, unusually, by two colons. Here, Jane's narration takes the reader deeper into her unhappiness. We are told that the now-impossible walk would, in any case, have been something unpleasant for her; that, while there was *no possibility* of going on one of their walks, she *never* enjoyed them anyway. The sentence is broken into three equated or explanatory sections which each stress Jane's sadness: first, she is glad not to go for a walk, not because she wants to do anything else but simply because she dislikes the walks themselves; second, she intensifies her expression of unhappiness in her statement that she dislikes walks 'especially on chilly afternoons such as this one'; third, she describes both how the companions on her walk make her feel sad and inferior, and that 'coming home' itself was 'dreadful'. In the sentence, Brontë adds one example after another of Jane's exclusion, of her being both a part of this household and yet 'at a distance' (l.17) or apart from it, just as, later, Jane describes the 'clear panes of glass, protecting, but not separating me from the drear November day' (ll.35–6).

The importance of the walk only becomes clear in the second paragraph. A cancelled walk seems a trivial point at which to start the novel; but, Brontë conveys three things through these opening two paragraphs: Jane's sense of a hostile natural world; her sensitive mind and physically weak body; and her alienation from, and to an extent her persecution at the hands of, Mrs Reed, her three children, and Bessie. Her thoughts about the walk illustrate how Jane is confined both by the physical world and also by the Reeds. Here, of course, lies the significance of her retreat to the window-seat and her immersion in a book later in the extract. Her resentment of the Reed children, alongside her physical inferiority, is conveyed by her bracketed report that they were 'for the time neither quarreling nor crying' (ll.14–15).

In the third paragraph, Jane's isolation is emphasised by her banishment from the 'cluster' of 'her darlings' around Mrs Reed, who is 'perfectly happy' as she lies 'reclined on a sofa by the fireside'. Jane, by contrast to the other children is 'dispensed' with, and, in contrast to the recumbent Mrs Reed, Jane sits cross-legged 'like a Turk', which is the first example of one of the novel's most interesting groups of figurative imagery. There is, for example, much talk of slavery in the novel, but no slaves. Similarly, there are many mentions of sultans, seraglios, and despots, but none of these is actually present in the book (for example, see Chapter 24). Which is to say that Brontë, from this moment on, draws imaginatively on several powerful and familiar images of otherness and oppression. Jane will be imagined and described in terms of outsider figures or heathens (such as the Turk) but will also be presented as a kind of 'saviour of oppressed peoples'. On the one hand, Jane is herself compared with 'a little heathen' (p.98) but, on the other, she dislikes 'Eastern allusions' to harems in connection with her (p.297) and at the same time says she will 'Go preach liberty to them that are enslaved'. In terms of its historical position, it is worth noting here that the novel was published after the abolition of slavery (via the Emancipation Act of 1834), but is set before it. Brontë is drawing on the moral language of the abolitionists, as had many campaigners for the causes of women and the working-class; this had the effect of relieving slavery of its racial significance but of increasing its emotional force on Europeans (for instance, the working-class struggle spoke of a 'white slavery'). Later, at Lowood school, Helen Burns chastises Jane for wanting to 'strike back': 'Heathens and savage tribes hold that doctrine; but Christians and civilised nations disown it.' (p.90). Also, when Helen passes by, Jane says: 'It was as if a martyr, a hero, had passed a slave or victim, and imparted strength in the transit.' (p.99). For Helen, Christian endurance means suffering in this life to reap the rewards of heaven; for Jane, it means being unfairly and unhappily positioned as akin to a slave or victim.

Jane's 'unhappiness' is also, supposedly, the reason why Mrs Reed withdraws 'privileges' from her; because she is not a 'contented, happy' child (l.22), and needs to be more 'sociable' and 'sprightly': 'lighter, franker, more natural'. One of the key terms in Mrs Reed's list of improvements is 'more ... child-like'. Mrs Reed dislikes Jane because she does not seem to be like her own children, and because she is capable of mature, adult reflection: she can answer back and ask questions herself. For Mrs Reed, there is 'something truly forbidding in a child taking up her elders in that manner' (ll.25–6), and this establishes the theme of rebellion and resistance that runs throughout the novel and characterises Jane's reaction to any injustice she perceives around her, in the promotion of her own rights or of women's equality, in her denunciation of Oriental despotism or patriarchy.

In the absence of holding any power in the Reed household, Jane is forced to retreat to the solitary confinement, or welcome solitude, of the breakfast-room. Here, like so many alienated fictional heroes and heroines, she sits and reads, mimicking at the start of the story the reader's own solitary involvement with the text. In her isolation and with the rain beating against the window next to her, Jane identifies with the sea-birds who alone inhabit 'the solitary rocks and promontories'. On the one hand, this further encourages the reader's identification with Jane as a rebellious Romantic figure, as a caged bird who longs to be free like the sea-birds. Many critics see in this a metaphor for the contemporary female reader contained by patriarchy and seeking emancipation (physically, like the slaves, and spiritually, like the 'heathens'). On the other hand, at least one reader, Gayatri Spivak, has characterised Jane's retreat into the breakfast room as part of a 'self-marginalised uniqueness' redolent of the ideology of bourgeois individualism. Other commentators have seen Jane's position in the window-seat as that of a small and orphaned child: a girl conscious of her 'physical inferiority' to other children, she has to 'mount' into the 'window-seat' and then curl herself up into a foetal position in the enclosed space between folds of scarlet drapery and the window. This range of commentaries, focusing respectively on Jane's position as a woman, a bourgeois imperial subject, or an orphan, underlies the flexibility of textual interpretation but also illustrates that the critic's reading is, necessarily if not always knowingly, as partial and ideologically shaped as the author's writing.

Further Reading

Eagleton, Terry (1975) *Myths of Power: A Marxist Study of the Brontës*, London: Macmillan – now Palgrave.

Jacobus, Mary (1986) *Reading Women: Essays in Feminist Criticism*, London: Methuen.

Kaplan, Cora (1986) *Sea-Changes: Essays in Culture and Feminism*, London: Verso.

Spivak, Gayatri (1986) 'Three Women's Texts and a Critique of Imperialism' in Henry Gates (ed.), *'Race', Writing, and Difference*, Chicago: University of Chicago Press.

Chapter 6

Emily Brontë
Wuthering Heights
(1847)

1801 – I have just returned from a visit to my landlord – the
solitary neighbour that I shall be troubled with. This is certainly
a beautiful country! In all England, I do not believe that I could
have fixed on a situation so completely removed from the stir of
society. A perfect misanthropist's Heaven – and Mr. Heathcliff   5
and I are such a suitable pair to divide the desolation between us.
A capital fellow! He little imagined how my heart warmed towards him when I beheld his black eyes withdraw so suspiciously
under their brows, as I rode up, and when his fingers sheltered
themselves, with a jealous resolution, still further in his waistcoat,   10
as I announced my name.

"Mr. Heathcliff?" I said.

A nod was the answer.

"Mr. Lockwood, your new tenant, sir – I do myself the honour
of calling as soon as possible after my arrival, to express the hope   15
that I have not inconvenienced you by my perseverance in solicit-
ing the occupation of Thrushcross Grange: I heard, yesterday,
you had had some thoughts –"

"Thrushcross Grange is my own, sir," he interrupted, wincing,
"I should not allow any one to inconvenience me, if I could   20
hinder it – walk in!"

The "walk in" was uttered with closed teeth and expressed
the sentiment, "Go to the Deuce!" Even the gate over which he
leant manifested no sympathizing movement to the words; and
I think that circumstance determined me to accept the invitation: 25
I felt interested in a man who seemed more exaggeratedly reserved than myself.

When he saw my horse's breast fairly pushing the barrier, he
did pull out his hand to unchain it, and then sullenly preceded
me up the causeway, calling, as we entered the court: 30

"Joseph, take Mr. Lockwood's horse; and bring up some wine."

"Here we have the whole establishment of domestics, I suppose," was the reflection suggested by the compound order.
"No wonder the grass grows up between the flags, and cattle are
the only hedge-cutters."   35
    Joseph was an elderly, nay, an old man: very old perhaps,
though hale and sinewy.
    "The Lord help us!" he soliloquised in an undertone of peevish
displeasure, while relieving me of my horse: looking, meantime,
in my face so sourly that I charitably conjectured he must have   40
need of divine aid to digest his dinner, and his pious ejaculation
had no reference to my unexpected advent.
    Wuthering Heights is the name of Mr. Heathcliff's dwelling,
"Wuthering" being a significant provincial adjective, descriptive
of the atmospheric tumult to which its station is exposed in   45
stormy weather. Pure, bracing ventilation they must have up
there, at all times, indeed: one may guess the power of the north
wind, blowing over the edge, by the excessive slant of a few,
stunted firs at the end of the house; and by a range of gaunt
thorns all stretching their limbs one way, as if craving alms of the 50
sun. Happily, the architect had foresight to build it strong: the
narrow windows are deeply set in the wall, and the corners
defended with large jutting stones.
    Before passing the threshold, I paused to admire a quantity of
grotesque carving lavished over the front, and especially about   55
the principal door, above which, among a wilderness of crumbling
griffins and shameless little boys, I detected the date "1500"
and the name "Hareton Earnshaw".
                    (Oxford: Oxford University Press, 1981, ed. Ian Jack)

The opening to *Wuthering Heights* introduces a number of oppositions and contrasts. There is that between the Heights and the
Grange, between 1801 and 1500, between misanthropy and socia-
bility, between a heaven and a hell, and between Heathcliff and the
narrator Lockwood. This last is not quickly perceived by Lockwood,
who considers himself and Heathcliff 'a suitable pair to divide the
desolation between us' (l.6). Lockwood is a city-dweller seeking rest
from 'the stir of society' (ll.4–5) and imagines himself to be similar to
his landlord. He soon finds, however, that his desire for temporary
seclusion is different from Heathcliff's refusal to 'allow anyone to
inconvenience me' (l.20). Lockwood has called on his landlord 'as
soon as possible' (l.15) after his arrival, suggesting a tendency to

socialise at odds with his stated feeling that Heathcliff is the 'solitary neighbour that I shall be troubled with' (1.2). Heathcliff is indeed 'solitary', but in a different sense, and Lockwood soon finds himself 'interested in a man who seemed more exaggeratedly reserved than myself' (ll.26–7).

Critics habitually analyse Brontë's novel in terms of contrasts, particularly that between the Heights and the Grange, the Earnshaws and the Lintons. I also want to consider oppositions in *Wuthering Heights*, but in terms of language, not character and location. To do this I will employ some of the concepts of the Russian critic Mikhail Bakhtin whose theories of the novel provide a distinctive approach to the analysis of textual meaning. My starting points from the opening pages of the novel, because their importance will also be evident in the conclusion of my analysis, are the two sentences: 'Thrushcross Grange is my own, sir' (1.19) and 'Wuthering Heights is the name of Mr. Heathcliff's dwelling' (1.43).

At the heart of Bakhtin's theories is the idea of dialogism. Bakhtin believed that nothing has meaning in itself but only in relation to something else. He is often misrepresented as someone who promoted *dialogic* discourse over *monologic* discourse, but he believed nothing could really be monologic, could be so powerful and authoritative that it ceased to be in dialogue with anything else. Nothing exists in a vacuum and discourse can only *tend towards* the monologic by trying to monopolise meaning, by denying other perspectives. All speech is still in dialogue with those discourses it attempts to dominate. For Bakhtin, dialogism is the study of the way meaning is constructed out of the contending discourses within any culture. Discourses are contending because there is always an authoritarian tendency to try to unify meanings within an official language: in other words, the dominant political forces in a society will continually seek to promote their language as the correct one, and will pressure language towards, without ever successfully arriving at, the monologic. Bakhtin believed language to be neither neutral or objective, but always involved with power and ideology in a particular situation. Language and its meanings for the most part are dominated by the ruling authorities, which means that subordinated classes necessarily use language subversively. Bakhtin was therefore less interested in the way that language reflects society than in the ways it can be made to disrupt authority and give voice to the underprivileged. Bakhtin considered all speech or writing to be involved in a discursive struggle because there is not one single language but a multiplicity of overlapping and often conflicting versions of that language: official, vernacular, technical, literary, religious and so on. David Lodge writes in *After Bakhtin* (1990: 22) that:

> There is an indissoluble link in Bakhtin's theory between the linguistic variety of prose fiction, which he called heteroglossia, and its cultural function as the continuous critique of all repressive, authoritarian, one-eyed ideologies. As soon as you allow a variety of discourses into a textual space – vulgar discourses as well as polite ones, vernacular as well as literary, oral as well as written – you establish a resistance ... to the dominance of any one discourse.

Bakhtin therefore roots meaning in the social, though the social is conceived in a special way because Bakhtin's concept of language is as something essentially dialogic: that is, the word is a two-sided act. The words we use come to us already imprinted with the intentions and accents of previous users, and the novel for Bakhtin is a mix of varying and opposed languages in which a number of different types of speech, representing different belief systems, carry out an unresolved battle. Fiction therefore presents a multiplicity of social voices and in studying a novel it is profitable to analyse the range of competing voices. Words have meanings according to the groups that use them and language is always in a state of flux: this potential of language to mean different things is the basis of Bakhtin's dialogism.

So, for Bakhtin there is always an official language in play; one which is generally accepted and sanctioned by society. With *Wuthering Heights*, it is possible from this perspective to interrogate the use of names inside and outside the text in terms of a struggle for power, property and possession; not between the Grange and the Heights but between those with and without privilege, those with being the dynastic patriarchs in the Linton and Earnshaw families, and those without being the women and orphans, particularly the first Cathy and Heathcliff.

First of all, names and narrators within and without *Wuthering Heights* seem to reinforce a masculine norm in society. For example, in 1847, the first fictional name a reader would have encountered (without knowing it) was the pseudonym under which Emily Brontë published the novel: 'Ellis Bell'. Additionally, the author 'Ellis Bell' employed a male character, Lockwood, as the principal narrating voice. From a Bakhtinian perspective this apparent male authority is undermined first by the fact that Ellis, though it is assumed by many readers to be a male name, is in fact an androgynous name, like Currer and Acton, the names chosen by Charlotte and Anne Brontë; and second, by the introduction of a female narrator, Nelly Dean, who in fact provides and controls the majority of the story that Lockwood tells.

If we next consider the names within the text itself, an initial puzzle is 'Heathcliff'. The character's position as orphan, or perhaps illegitimate son, is reinforced by the lack of an additional name. 'Heathcliff' stands as both first name and surname, but it is at first used only as a forename and therefore an emasculated Heathcliff lacks the father's surname which would represent his masculine power and identity in a property-owning society. This allies his socio-economic position with that of women in 1847, who could neither own property in marriage nor pass on their surname to a child. However, this is undermined by the history of the name that the orphan is given: 'Heathcliff' was the name of the Earnshaws' dead first son, and this connection implies that the illegitimate Heathcliff has a nominal right to inherit the family wealth. It is also an important semantic point that the name 'Heathcliff' has a similar meaning to the name of the Earnshaws' house. Lockwood informs the reader in the opening that: '"Wuthering" being a significant provincial adjective, descriptive of the atmospheric tumult to which its station is exposed in stormy weather.' (ll.44–6). Similarly, the name 'Heathcliff' connotes a lofty windswept place, adding further meaning to Lockwood's previous observation that: 'Wuthering Heights is the name of Mr. Heathcliff's dwelling' (l.43).

Another important example, if we consider the main female character, occurs when Lockwood reads Cathy's carving on his window ledge at the Heights at the start of Chapter 3. The names he reads are in this order: Catherine Earnshaw, Catherine Heathcliff and Catherine Linton. These names trace the transitions of the first Catherine's life from her father's 'possession' to her love for Heathcliff, to her marriage to Edgar Linton. While she takes the names of the other two men, the shift to the name 'Heathcliff' never actually occurs of course, except in Catherine's famous assertion 'I *am* Heathcliff' (p.82). There is then a sense in which 'Catherine Heathcliff' is aborted at the moment Heathcliff runs away from the Heights. The name 'Catherine Heathcliff', as far as the first Cathy is concerned, never exists except as a warning to the families: a potential threat to the dynasties of the Earnshaws and the Lintons through the union of two disinherited first names. This name-that-never-was seems additionally to function as a premonition of the disruption that happens later in the novel.

On the first Catherine's death the book goes into reverse and her daughter is born Catherine Linton, then takes the name Heathcliff, and finally becomes a second Catherine Earnshaw by marrying Hindley. The union of the second Catherine with Heathcliff's family is again a wedge driven between the Earnshaws and the Lintons. In terms of Bakhtin's idea of language as a 'power struggle', another significant aspect to the novel is the struggle over the names of mother and daughter. They are both called Catherine, and this fact makes both their names a battlezone for Edgar and Heathcliff. For example, in Volume 2, Chapter 3, we are told this of the second Catherine's birth: 'It was named Catherine, but [Edgar] never called it the name in full, as he had never called the first Catherine short, probably because Heathcliff had a habit of doing so.' (p.183). Consequently, the choice that even the reader makes in calling each of the women by either of the names betrays an allegiance to either Edgar or Heathcliff.

Lastly, and most importantly for a reading of the situation at the start of the novel, Heathcliff is, as I have said, introduced as an orphan (like Jane Eyre), and he is therefore in a sense placed in a female position because he does not have the rights of patrimonial inheritance of a male child. The name he is then given is only a single name which serves at first as a forename lacking a family name. Heathcliff, who is never given any second name and in this sense a whole name or identity, in order to recover his place in patriarchy spends the second half of the novel acquiring status through the spread of his name, which he transforms into a surname, his own family name, and through marriage he gains the property he desires and he also forces his 'singular' name on others. 'Heathcliff' becomes a powerful surname and one which threatens to engulf both 'Linton' and 'Earnshaw'. In the second half of the novel he also creates the 'Catherine Heathcliff' identity that was earlier denied by marrying the second Catherine to his son Linton (he has appropriated the dynastic name in order to rule over it). The name Linton may therefore die out, and Heathcliff's revenge is completed by the fact that he has made 'Linton' into no more than a powerless forename like his own once was.

A further way of considering the struggle over meanings in the book is in terms of eschatology. This is important because Heathcliff ultimately loses interest in his earthly battle with the Earnshaws and the Lintons, not just because he defeats all his opponents but because he shifts his struggle to another arena: heaven and hell, where he can try once more to fight for the love and possession of the first Catherine. Appropriately, therefore, the opening has several references to religion, but none is clearcut, from the paradoxical 'misanthropist's Heaven' (l.5) to the exclamations 'Go to the Deuce!' (l.23) and 'The Lord help us!' (l.38). Such figures of speech are present throughout the novel and suggest the opposition of the mythological world of the moors, with its fairies, sprites and griffins (l.57), to the revered holy places of traditional religion. Such contrasts are embodied in the irascible Joseph, the zealot who speaks the Lord's name while 'looking, meantime, in my face so sourly that I charitably conjectured he must have need of divine aid to digest his dinner, and his pious ejaculation had no reference to my unexpected advent' (ll.39–42). In *Wuthering Heights* there is a constant battle over the notions of heaven and hell. When Heathcliff first sees the Grange he says that he and the first Cathy would be in heaven if they had the comforts of Edgar and Isabella. Similarly, when the first Cathy dies, Heathcliff repeatedly says he is in hell. Towards the end, he again states that heaven would be a reunion with Cathy: he talks of a hell on earth without her and a clearly non-Christian heaven in the grave with her. This is juxtaposed with orthodox views of heaven and hell such as Joseph's and Lockwood's dream of the Reverend Jabes Branderham and sins. The contrast is brought out by the discussion between Linton and the second Cathy. Linton pictures heaven as a quiet peaceful idyll, while the second Cathy sees it as a tempestuous, windswept landscape such as the moors. In terms of a Bakhtinian contest for meaning, this again enacts a struggle between an accepted, authoritative, official version and an underprivileged, subversive one.

In conclusion, the last words of the opening I have quoted are: 'Before passing the threshold, I paused to admire a quantity of grotesque carving lavished over the front, and especially about the principal door, above which, among a wilderness of crumbling griffins and shameless little boys, I detected the date "1500" and the name "Hareton Earnshaw"' (ll.54–8). In terms of names, and their symbolization of power struggles, as in other ways, *Wuthering Heights* has a cyclical shape. Hareton Earnshaw is the name of the builder of the Heights and it is a new Hareton Earnshaw who, by marrying the second Catherine, born a Linton, brings the novel full circle, by possessing the Heights again. Meanwhile, Heathcliff, the orphan who has become the catalyst and engineer of the book's *revolutions*, has turned away from this secular struggle to a supernatural battle over 'heaven' and 'hell'.

Further Reading

Lodge, David (1990) *After Bakhtin: Essays on Fiction and Criticism*, London: Routledge.

Miles, Peter (1990) *Wuthering Heights*, London: Macmillan – now Palgrave.

Musselwhite, David E. (1987) *Partings Welded Together: Politics and Desire in the Nineteenth-Century English Novel*, London: Methuen.

Chapter 7

Charles Dickens
Great Expectations
(1861)

My father's family name being Pirrip, and my christian name
Philip, my infant tongue could make of both names nothing longer
or more explicit than Pip. So, I called myself Pip, and came to be
called Pip.

I give Pirrip as my father's family name, on the authority of his   5
tombstone and my sister – Mrs Joe Gargery, who married the
blacksmith. As I never saw my father or my mother, and never saw
any likeness of either of them (for their days were long before the
days of photographs), my first fancies regarding what they were
like, were unreasonably derived from their tombstones. The shape   10
of the letters on my father's, gave me an odd idea that he was a
square, stout, dark man, with curly black hair. From the character
and turn of the inscription, *'Also Georgiana Wife of the Above,'* I
drew a childish conclusion that my mother was freckled and sickly.
To five little stone lozenges, each about a foot and a half long,   15
which were arranged in a neat row beside their grave, and were
sacred to the memory of five little brothers of mine – who gave up
trying to get a living, exceedingly early in the universal struggle –
I am indebted for a belief I religiously entertained that they had
all been born on their backs with their hands in their trousers-   20
pockets, and had never taken them out in this state of existence.

Ours was the marsh country, down by the river, within, as the
river wound, twenty miles of the sea. My first most vivid and broad
impression of the identity of things, seems to me to have been
gained on a memorable raw afternoon towards evening. At such   25
a time I found out for certain, that this bleak place overgrown with
nettles was the churchyard; and that Philip Pirrip, late of this
parish, and also Georgiana wife of the above, were dead and
buried; and that Alexander, Bartholomew, Abraham, Tobias, and
Roger, infant children of the aforesaid, were also dead and buried;   30
and that the dark flat wilderness beyond the churchyard, intersected

with dykes and mounds and gates, with scattered feeding on
it, was the marshes; and that the low leaden line beyond, was the
river; and that the distant savage lair from which the wind was
rushing, was the sea; and that the small bundle of shivers growing   35
afraid of it all and beginning to cry, was Pip.

'Hold your noise!' cried a terrible voice, as a man started up
from among the graves at the side of the church porch. 'Keep still,
you little devil, or I'll cut your throat!'

A fearful man, all in coarse grey, with a great iron on his leg. A   40
man with no hat, and with broken shoes, and with an old rag tied
round his head. A man who had been soaked in water, and
smothered in mud, and lamed by stones, and cut by flints, and
stung by nettles, and torn by briars; who limped, and shivered, and
glared and growled; and whose teeth chattered in his head as he   45
seized me by the chin.

'O! Don't cut my throat, sir,' I pleaded in terror. 'Pray don't do
it, sir.'

'Tell us your name!' said the man. 'Quick!'

'Pip, sir.'   50

'Once more,' said the man, staring at me. 'Give it mouth!'

'Pip. Pip, sir.'

'Show us where you live,' said the man. 'Pint out the place!'

I pointed to where our village lay, on the flat in-shore
among the alder trees and pollards, a mile or more from the   55
church.

The man, after looking at me for a moment, turned me upside
down, and emptied my pockets.

(Harmondsworth: Penguin, 1965)

There are several clues to the novel's major concerns in this opening.
To begin with, the issue of identity is present in several ways. There
is Pip's reduction of his two names to one syllable, his abandoned
status as an orphan, and the fact that he does not even know what
his parents or his brothers looked like. He is in many respects a child
cut off from his roots, in family, heritage and language. Towards the
end of these opening paragraphs, two important things happen.
First, Pip comes to consciousness of the composition of the world
('this ... was the churchyard ... that ... the marshes ... that ... the
river ... that ... the sea': (ll.26–35) and his own place within it: 'My
first most vivid and broad impression of the *identity* of things, seems
to me to have been gained on a memorable raw afternoon towards

evening. At such a time I found out for certain ... that the small bundle of shivers growing afraid of it all and beginning to cry, was Pip.' (ll.25–36; my emphasis). It is also at this moment, when Pip comes to his first real understanding of his identity, that the escaped convict Magwitch appears with the command, 'Tell us your name!'(l.49) It is of course the interference of Magwitch in Pip's life that will cause him to change his identity from blacksmith's boy to London gentleman, to grow from this barely self-aware seed or 'pip' into the sophisticated narrator who recounts the story.

It is also appropriate that the novel starts with this beginning in terms of genre. *Great Expectations* is, like Brontë's *Jane Eyre* (see earlier discussion), a *Bildungsroman*: a novel of the growth of a person's character and understanding from childhood to maturity. *Great Expectations* is also a novel of the comic grotesque, and this is apparent in the opening. Consider, for example, the way in which Magwitch 'start[s] up from among the graves' (l.38) as though he has come back to life; and, in the same vein, Magwitch unnecessarily scares himself a page later when Pip informs him that his parents are 'there' in the churchyard. Similarly grotesque is the description of Magwitch, which is far too detailed for Pip to have remembered and reads like a paragraph from a fairy story. Magwitch appears as someone 'soaked in water, and smothered in mud, and lamed by stones, and cut by flints, and stung by nettles, and torn by briars; who limped, and shivered, and glared and growled' (ll.42–5). Magwitch thus pops up like an angry but ultimately grateful genie (best known from the *One Thousand and One Nights*) and he will later make Pip's dreams come true (notice the way Pip presents Magwitch's appearance from his young self's perspective, making the convict's intrusion all the more sudden by omitting a verb from his sentence: 'A fearful man, all in coarse grey, with a great iron on his leg': l.40). However, Magwitch's initial outburst is less reminiscent of a genie than a goblin or evil monster in a fairy tale: 'Hold your noise! ... Keep still, you little devil, or I'll cut your throat!' (ll.37–9). In a manner fitting to his treatment at his sister's house, as soon as Pip becomes fully aware of his 'self' and starts to cry (l.36), he is told to shut up.

The fantasy aspect to the story is evident in the roles of characters such as Mrs Joe and Miss Havisham who to an extent play the traditional fairy tale parts of wicked stepmother and fairy godmother to the orphan Pip. This can be expanded to the other characters: Wemmick as nobleman in his drawbridged 'Castle', Joe as good angel, Jaggers as all-powerful conjuring wizard. The influence of

Romance is also there in the basic plot of a quest for love in the mysterious and seemingly unattainable princess-figure of Estella whom Pip thinks he must win by becoming a gentleman. The comic grotesque elements surface frequently in Dickens's descriptions, such as the goblin at the window sill at the start of Chapter 3 or the image of Miss Havisham's decayed wedding feast.

Appropriately for a serialised novel, the opening poses questions that maintain the reader's interest by creating a sense of suspense. After the initial mystery over the unknown convict, the narrative continues to bristle with unresolved, and often interrelated, questions: Who is Pip's benefactor? Who was the small boy Pip met at Satis House? Who are Estella's parents? What is the identity of Jaggers's housekeeper? Who was the young man with Magwitch in the graveyard? Such narrative puzzles of identity invoke issues of disguise and transformation which are also mirrored at several levels in changes in names. As we see from the opening sentence of the book, names will be important, and indeed names do proliferate in the book: Pip = boy = Handel ('harmonious blacksmith'); Magwitch = Provis; Orlick = 'wolf'; Drummle = 'the spider', and so on. The book will similarly, in fairy-tale fashion, transform the characters' relationships with each other. For example, the 'young gentleman' with whom he fights reappears as Pip's room-mate Herbert; not Miss Havisham but Magwitch turns out to be Pip's benefactor; it was the young man with Magwitch, Compeyson, who jilted Miss Havisham on her wedding day; Estella proves to be Magwitch's, and Jaggers's housekeeper's, daughter. All these are variations on the central story of Pip's change from blacksmith's boy to rich fop: it is a world turned upside-down and shaken up in this opening scene, by Magwitch. Pip's literal inversion by Magwitch is recreated by Magwitch later turning upside-down Pip's notion of what 'makes' a gentleman. Through such symbolic and unexpected events, Dickens puts the accepted notions of money, class, and manners into play with those of a different set of characters: blacksmiths, convicts, and poor relations.

One of Dickens's greatest strengths is his ability to blend the grotesque and the comic with social comment. For example, many readers complain about the coincidences in his novels, such as when it transpires that Magwitch is not only Pip's benefactor but also Estella's father. If we think about this problem slightly differently, in terms of narrative, then it seems an economical way of emphasising a point. Here, as elsewhere, Dickens is interrogating the superficiality of the class system, and the influence of parents on children (note the opening paragraph's immediate concern with fathers, and kinds of inheritance, from names to money: a recurring theme of the book). One of the novel's great ironies is that Pip thinks Estella will spurn him if she discovers Magwitch is his adopted parent, and yet Magwitch is Estella's biological parent. This is an ironic comment on snobbery which could have been made by introducing other characters but the point is made so much more succinctly by using only Magwitch, even if the coincidence does not conform to our experience of probability. A similar effect is achieved by the unlikely plot device of Magwitch making Pip, whom he barely knows, into a gentleman. The underlying point may be taken to be that social standing, including that of Pip's gentility, is supported by labour and trade, by Magwitch's colonial success and not by the fiscal patronage of Miss Havisham and the upper classes.

Dickens's comment on gentility and good manners is two-fold. On the one hand a 'true gentleman' cannot be bought and made, as Magwitch attempts with Pip – unless the individual is a gentleman at heart the result will be a snob ashamed of his background. As Herbert informs Pip: 'no man who was not a true gentleman at heart, ever was, since the world began, a true gentleman in manner' (p.204). On the other hand, a 'true' gentlewoman cannot be constructed and trained, as Miss Havisham attempts with Estella: the result is someone cold and unkind, disciplined but heartless. Both Pip and Estella after their grooming conform to society's view of sophisticated gentility, but neither meets Dickens's criterion of 'gentleness', found in the simple care and open kindness of Joe and Biddy.

This point highlights the significance of this opening scene, of an 'innocent' boy meeting a 'guilty' criminal amid his dead relatives, positioned between society and heredity at the first crossroads of his life. In contrast to the quality of true gentility, a personal characteristic fostered by a good 'heart' and conscience, the burden of 'guilt' is socially controlled. From this opening, in which he is watched by Magwitch, Pip is continually spied on or watched over: by his sister, by his relatives at the dinner table, and even by the cows beside the road on his journey to the churchyard. Each one accuses him of something: viciousness, ingratitude or theft. This point is crucial as the novel interrogates the subjective element in any label, such as 'thief'. Pip at this early stage of life has already identified himself with the role of guilty criminal and is beginning literally to 'see' himself as akin to Magwitch (who, ironically given Pip's later snobbery, is affected by the boy's innocence and his 'natural' kindness).

This identification is caused not just by the theft of the 'wittles', because Pip perceives a similarity through the witting and unwitting comparisons Mrs Gargery makes between him and convicts, even down to 'eating too much'. When Pip asks his sister why people are sent to the prison ships in Chapter 2, she replies that it is because they have done one of three things that stem from a fourth: murder, forgery and theft, all of which begin with asking too many questions. All these four apply to Pip: Mrs Joe tells Pip that he will be the 'death of her' which, added to the death of his parents and brothers, inevitably weighs on Pip's conscience. Theft is, we discover, what Pip is about to embark upon in stealing a pie and bottle for Magwitch. If convicts always start, says Mrs Gargery, 'by asking questions' (p.46), as Pip does, that at least leaves Pip free from the crime of forgery. But forgery is actually at the heart of the story, as Pip becomes an imitation or forged gentleman, which is in many ways portrayed later as a crime, against Joe and Biddy, and against the natural kindness he exhibited as a boy. Additionally, what Dickens suggests in deliberately using the word 'forgery' is that the proper place for this activity is in the blacksmith's forge where elements are brought harmoniously together, and not in London where the principal forging is concerned with money and deception.

Lastly, we need to say a word on Dickens's technique with regard to character, in which key elements are his use of parallels and juxtapositions. Most major aspects of the novel are repeated in smaller instances, images or symbols: Miss Havisham's decayed and disintegrating life is reflected in the rotten wedding cake centre-piece in the dining room of Satis House; Pip's change in character when he travels from Kent to London is mimicked in Wemmick's daily transformations between the roles of impersonal professional clerk and devoted son. Dickens also constantly imitates people's personalities in the objects they own, in their professions, and in their physical attributes. I will give three examples, one of each kind: the prickly and rampaging Mrs Joe habitually wears a 'square impenetrable [apron] stuck with pins and needles'; the child-hating Pumblechook who takes Pip to the closed airless world of Satis House is a cornchandler who keeps seedlings (pips) stifled in a drawer; the allpowerful lawyer Jaggers has enormous hands with which he is often described as gripping Pip's shoulder. Details such as these are part of Dickens's conception of a complete character in fiction whose every aspect reflects their personality. In this light, it is worth noting that Dickens often provides alternative types in his character portrayals, such that there are two convicts at the start, a poor man and a rich man; there are two contrasting blacksmiths, Joe and Orlick; and there are even the two sides to Wemmick, at home and work. All of which suggests that there are always two possibilities for, and two sides to any person. At the start of the novel, Pip has only just become aware of his 'identity' and, whatever expectations he or those around him have of his future, he will come to learn both that what he 'is' is more important than what he may 'become', and that while people place great store by the distinction between the two labels, the 'criminal' and the 'gentleman' are in many ways dependent upon each other in society. This is the knowledge brought to the text by the narrator Pip, who speaks with an adult's voice but for most of the book presents things from the perspective of his younger self.

Further Reading

Connor, Steven (ed.) (1996) *Charles Dickens*, Harlow: Longman.
Gilmour, Robin (1981) *The Idea of the Gentleman in the Victorian Novel*, London: Allen & Unwin.
Hollington, Michael (1984) *Dickens and the Grotesque*, London: Croom Helm.

George Eliot
Silas Marner
(1861)

In the days when the spinning-wheels hummed busily in the
farmhouses – and even great ladies, clothed in silk and thread-
lace, had their toy spinning-wheels of polished oak – there
might be seen, in districts far away among the lanes, or deep in
the bosom of the hills, certain pallid undersized men, who, by   5
the side of the brawny country-folk, looked like the remnants of
a disinherited race. The shepherd's dog barked fiercely when
one of these alien-looking men appeared on the upland, dark
against the early winter sunset; for what dog likes a figure bent
under a heavy bag? – and these pale men rarely stirred abroad   10
without that mysterious burden. The shepherd himself, though
he had good reason to believe that the bag held nothing but
flaxen thread, or else the long rolls of strong linen spun from
that thread, was not quite sure that this trade of weaving, indis-
pensable though it was, could be carried on entirely without the   15
help of the Evil One. In that far-off time superstition clung
easily round every person or thing that was at all unwonted, or
even intermittent and occasional merely, like the visits of the
pedlar or the knife-grinder. No one knew where wandering men
had their homes or their origin; and how was a man to be   20
explained unless you at least knew somebody who knew his
father and mother? To the peasants of old time, the world outside their own direct experience was a region of vagueness and
mystery: to their untravelled thought a state of wandering was a
conception as dim as the winter life of the swallows that came   25
back with the spring; and even a settler, if he came from distant
parts, hardly ever ceased to be viewed with a remnant of distrust, which would have prevented any surprise if a long course
of inoffensive conduct on his part had ended in the commission
of a crime; especially if he had any reputation for knowledge, or   30
showed any skill in handicraft. All cleverness, whether in the

rapid use of that difficult instrument the tongue, or in some
other art unfamiliar to villagers, was in itself suspicious: honest
folks, born and bred in a visible manner, were mostly not overwise or clever – at least, not beyond such a matter as knowing   35
the signs of the weather; and the process by which rapidity and
dexterity of any kind were acquired was so wholly hidden, that
they partook of the nature of conjuring. In this way it came to
pass that those scattered linen-weavers – emigrants from the
town into the country – were to the last regarded as aliens by   40
their rustic neighbours, and usually contracted the eccentric
habits which belong to a state of loneliness.

                                        (Harmondsworth: Penguin, 1996)

In terms of style, this opening paragraph usefully illustrates Eliot's
rhythmic, graceful sentences. Several of these contain asides or
passing comments after dashes, but the sense of continuity is also
evident in the constancy of subject: wandering men. Each sentence
follows clearly from the previous one as the narrator guides us
through a number of points about these outsiders and the attitudes
adopted to them by shepherds, farmers, and other peasants. The
sentences are generally long – one exceeds a hundred words – and
contain several subclauses, but they are not difficult to follow.
Unlike the convoluted sentences found in the late style of Henry
James, for example, Eliot's contain more progression than digression
and the reader is in no real danger of losing track of them. What is
apparent, however, is the presence of an all-knowing, confident,
authoritative narrator. This is usually taken to be Eliot's voice, as
Jane Austen's narrators are often taken to be the author herself, but
this in no way prevents the reader from assessing the kind of narrator and the style of narrative present in the novel. Typical of
realism, Eliot adopts a 'hierarchy of discourse', which is to say that
instead of speaking in the first person as an individual with her own
views amongst the views of others, she uses a third-person narrator
whose opinions are authoritative, whose statements are truthful, and
whose knowledge, reliability and trustworthiness are taken for
granted – which cannot be said of any of the characters in the novel.
In other words, the narrator sits above the rest of the figures in the
novel; unlike them she is omnipresent, omniscient, and even
omnipotent: the author/narrator as God. In the world of the novel,
she may contradict any statement, or even thought, made by any
character, but because the narrator is not one of them, none of the

characters will ever pass comment on, or be aware of, her mediation of the story. Thus the narrator is located on a different plane from the characters or from the reader and author: nothing can be known of the narrator and no interaction can take place because she, or he, is just a disembodied voice. While the material is transmuted into the genre of the novel, the model used here is, broadly speaking, that of journalism and historiography, in which an authoritative voice explains events in the lives of others in a similarly unbiased and truthful way, except that, in these other forms of writing, the person speaking in the text is recognised as the author, and this is someone identifiable and accountable. However, in realist fiction, the figure of the omniscient narrator has become so familiar as a device that it does not occur to the reader to ask who the narrator is, unless the narrator is identified with the author. The narrator is both all-knowing and completely unknown.

The vocabulary of this opening is also worth commenting on in terms of kinds of narrative. Occasionally the language slips into a Biblical turn of phrase, as with 'it came to pass', while the debt to folk tales is apparent at the beginning of several sentences, such as 'In the days when' and 'In that far-off time'. The suggestion is not of 'fairy tales' but of fables and the style of medieval Romance, which will be juxtaposed in the narrative with the idioms and lexicon of realism, as in the phrases 'a long course of inoffensive conduct' and 'the process by which rapidity and dexterity of any kind were acquired' (ll.27, 36), to create a sense of different worlds, like the contrasting groups at the start of the text: the 'brawny country folk' and the 'alien-looking men' (ll.6, 8).

The extract begins with the distancing phrase 'In the days when ...', and Eliot's narrator clearly takes care to talk about superstition in terms of 'old' and 'far-off' times but says in her final sentence that 'those scattered linen-weavers – emigrants from the town into the country – were to the last regarded as aliens by their rustic neighbours'. And this leads the narrative in to a discussion of the present and the linen-weaver of the title. So, it will only be after Eliot's long opening paragraph that the novel's protagonist, Silas Marner, will be introduced along with the time period of the novel, the early 1800s. However, the themes of the novel have been carefully laid out in these first few dozen lines: loneliness, superstition, travelling, distrust of strangers, and fears of unfamiliar skills, eloquence and knowledge. The paragraph, which has twice mentioned the concept of the 'alien', ends with a statement of the 'loneliness' which for most of the book will characterise Silas's life. Superstition has been mentioned (l.16), along with the 'Evil One', and suspicions of 'conjuring'. The lives of itinerant travellers are alluded to as 'wandering men' such as the 'pedlar' and 'the knife-grinder', those whose professions require a larger number of customers than any one village could provide. Fears of anyone skilled in 'that difficult instrument the tongue' or 'art' are noted, because 'honest folks' are usually not 'overwise' or 'clever'. Distrust of strangers runs through the paragraph from the dog barking at 'alien-looking men' under a 'mysterious burden' to the central sentence: 'No one knew where wandering men had their homes or their origin; and how was a man to be explained unless you at least knew somebody who knew his father and mother?' Other themes are evident in the passage, even if they are presented only implicitly, such as the differences and connections across social groups or classes obliquely suggested by the first sentence where the farming families and the 'great ladies' are joined by their ownership of spinning-wheels, suggesting that Eliot's major symbol for the web that unites all members of a community will be thread, just as her principal character will be a weaver.

Silas's own experience is directly anticipated in the phrase: 'even a settler, if he came from distant parts, hardly ever ceased to be viewed with a remnant of distrust'; and when Silas is robbed, blame is almost automatically placed on the one figure, a pedlar, who travels through the village (Chapter 8). The other main suspect is Silas himself, even though he has been in the community many years, simply because, on the one hand, he was not born in the village, and on the other, he is not sociable: an unflagging scepticism about any outsider anticipated and underlined in this opening paragraph by the fact that it would have caused no 'surprise if a long course of inoffensive conduct on his part had ended in the commission of a crime'. Yet the novel will suggest that it is the communities which harbour these fears and suspicions that breed individuals capable of betrayal (at Lantern Yard) and dishonesty (at Raveloe). Eliot is concerned with showing how communities fail to extend to others the Christian principles they supposedly live by, and ascribe guilt to strangers while turning a blind eye to the failings of their own kind.

The beginning to the story thus works with certain kinds of binary opposition, not least in the depiction of two kinds of people: the 'pallid, undersized men' who appear 'the remnants of a disinherited race' and the 'brawny country-folk', a divison traced from the 'old times' when peasants thought of the lives of 'wandering men' as being as alien to them as 'the winter life of swallows that came back with the spring'. The division between an older 'race' who are 'undersized' and a newer one who are 'brawny' indicates Eliot's Darwinian world-view of change through the survival of the fittest, as kinds of trade or worker become extinct in the same way that species do. Such contrasts between one kind of world or people and another work throughout the novel, as at the start of the second paragraph of Chapter 2 when the reader is asked: 'And what could be more unlike the Lantern Yard world than the world in Raveloe?'

The opening's juxtaposition of genres and their accompanying world-views is repeated in the two plots developed by the narrative: while Silas's loss of his money and discovery of Eppie has the simple qualities of a fable, the story with which it is contrasted and increasingly intertwined, involving Dunstan and Godfrey Cass, is an example of the involved and detailed social realism more usually associated with Eliot's novels. For this novel, however, her combination of narrative styles grew directly out of the story's original idea, which 'came to me first of all, quite suddenly, as a sort of legendary tale, suggested by my recollection of having once, in early childhood, seen a linen-weaver with a bag on his back; but, as my mind dwelt on the subject, I became inclined to a more realistic treatment' (letter to John Blackwood, 24 February 1861). In *Silas Marner*, this fusion of narrative styles, broadly speaking realism and folk tale, implies Eliot's overarching message of the story: of the need sympathetically to reintroduce a knowledge of the complexity of human interdependency, represented by the involved story of the Cass family, into the simplicity of religion, symbolised by the parable of a child leading a persecuted man away from misanthropy and money towards love and redemption. Here, Eliot's conception of religion is indebted to that of the philosopher Ludwig Feuerbach, whose most famous book, *The Essence of Christianity* (1841), she translated. In Feuerbach's theory, religion is understood in human, natural terms rather than supernatural ones, and is considered to arise from the individual's alienation from self, such that 'God' is a projection of ideal human qualities on to an invented, all-powerful being.

In conclusion, at the most straightforward structural level, the opening brings out the binaries of class, belief, genre and the familiar against the unfamiliar (in terms of people, knowledge and skill) that will be developed in the rest of the book. The two plots of the novel, involving Silas (and also the community at Lantern Yard) on the one hand and the Cass family (and the world of Raveloe) on the other, also suggest how *Silas Marner* would be amenable to readings which focus on binary oppositions and their subversion. The tensions of the novel work at the level of the characters' lives, at the level of world-views (human-centred explanations and supernatural ones) and at the level of form, where realism stands alongside fable.

Further Reading

Beer, Gillian (1983) *Darwin's Plots*, London: Routledge.
Dentith, Simon (1986) *George Eliot*, Brighton: Harvester.
Newton, K.M. (ed.) (1990) *George Eliot*, Harlow: Longman.

Thomas Hardy
Tess of the D'Urbervilles
(1891)

On an evening in the latter part of May a middle-aged man was
walking homeward from Shaston to the village of Marlott, in
the adjoining Vale of Blakemore or Blackmoor. The pair of
legs that carried him were rickety, and there was a bias in his
gait which inclined him somewhat to the left of a straight line.   5
He occasionally gave a smart nod, as if in confirmation of some
opinion, though he was not thinking of anything in particular.
An empty egg-basket was slung upon his arm, the nap of his
hat was ruffled, a patch being quite worn away at its brim
where his thumb came in taking it off. Presently he was met   10
by an elderly parson astride on a gray mare, who, as he rode,
hummed a wandering tune.

'Good night t'ee,' said the man with the basket.

'Good night, Sir John,' said the parson.

The pedestrian, after another pace or two, halted, and turned   15
round.

'Now, sir, begging your pardon; we met last market-day on
this road about this time, and I zaid "Good night", and you
made reply "*Good night, Sir John*", as now.'

'I did,' said the parson.   20

'And once before that – near a month ago.'

'I may have.'

'Then what might your meaning be in calling me "Sir John"
these different times, when I be plain Jack Durbeyfield, the
haggler?'   25

The parson rode a step or two nearer.

'It was only my whim,' he said; and, after a moment's hesi-
tation: 'It was on account of a discovery I made some little
time ago, whilst I was hunting up pedigrees for the new county
history. I am Parson Tringham, the antiquary, of Stagfoot Lane.   30
Don't you really know, Durbeyfield, that you are the lineal

representative of the ancient and knightly family of the
d'Urbervilles, who derive their descent from Sir Pagan d'Urberville, that renowned knight who came from Normandy with
William the Conqueror, as appears by Battle Abbey Roll?'   35
   'Never heard it before, sir!'
   'Well it's true. Throw up your chin a moment, so that I may
catch the profile of your face better. Yes, that's the d'Urberville nose and chin – a little debased. Your ancestor was one of
the twelve knights who assisted the Lord of Estremavilla in   40
Normandy in his conquest of Glamorganshire. Branches of your
family held manors over all this part of England; their names
appear in the Pipe Rolls in the time of King Stephen. In the
reign of King John one of them was rich enough to give a manor
to the Knights Hospitallers; and in Edward the Second's time   45
your forefather Brian was summoned to Westminster to attend
the great Council there. You declined a little in Oliver Crom-
well's time, but to no serious extent, and in Charles the
Second's reign you were made Knights of the Royal Oak for
your loyalty. Aye, there have been generations of Sir Johns   50
among you, and if knighthood were hereditary, like a baronetcy,
as it practically was in old times, when men were knighted
from father to son, you would be Sir John now.'
   'Ye don't say so!'
   'In short,' concluded the parson, decisively smacking his leg   55
with his switch, 'there's hardly such another family in England.'
   'Daze my eyes, and isn't there?' said Durbeyfield. 'And here
have I been knocking about, year after year, from pillar to post,
as if I was no more than the commonest feller in the parish ...'
                                   (Harmondsworth: Penguin, 1978)

As with Hardy's next and last novel, *Jude the Obscure, Tess of the
D'Urbervilles* begins at a defining moment without which the subsequent events might never have happened. It is in this sense that
Hardy's beginning is the origin, or at least a starting-point, of Tess's
story. The opening provides the catalyst for Tess Durbeyfield's transformation into Tess of the d'Urbervilles, the importance of which is
conveyed in the names themselves. The surname Durbey*field* suggests a land-based family, while d'Urberville implies either a family
of the urban and the town (*ville* is, of course, still French for town) or a
transition to the city from the village, which is a late medieval word
from the French *village,* and derived like many other words from the

Latin *villa* (a *ville*in was a peasant personally bound to a lord to whom dues and services were paid in return for land). In this way Hardy signals the 'ache of modernism' (Chapter 19) that many critics consider the main theme of the book: a transition from the communal life of the land towards the world of the anonymous teeming crowds of the city.

The opening suggests the combined influence of two forces on the Durbeyfields: the clergy and the aristocracy. The parson nearly does not tell what he has learned to John Durbeyfield but in doing so clearly gives him ideas above his station by linking him to an 'ancient and knightly family'. The history of the Durbeyfields is immediately placed in the lineage of Norman knights who came from France with William the Conqueror to subdue the English in 1066. The d'Urbervilles are descended from Sir Pagan, a name which implies a link with the pre-Christian nature cults which will be associated with Tess, who opposes and is opposed by the rules of the Church throughout the novel (for example, Tess's baby is buried 'in the shabby corner of God's allotment where He lets the nettles grow, and where all ... the conjecturally damned are laid': Chapter 14). Tess is an expression for Hardy of a human being in tune with nature and not with human institutions:

> On these lonely hills and dales her quiescent glide was of a piece with the element she moved in. Her flexuous and stealthy figure became an integral part of the scene. At times her whimsical fancy would intensify natural processes around her till they seemed a part of her own story. (Chapter 13)

So from this opening the novel establishes an opposition between, on the one hand, the land, nature and villagers like the Durbeyfields, and on the other the clergy, aristocracy and the forces of urbanisation. The novel's inaugural moment throws these two worlds together when Jack Durbeyfield the haggler is hailed as 'Sir John'. In this he is distracted from his normal course of life into thinking of himself as a different person from the one who has 'been knocking about, year after year, from pillar to post, as if I was no more than the commonest feller in the parish' (ll.58–9). The possibility of Durbeyfield being 'led astray' in this way is suggested in the second sentence of the novel when he is described thus: 'there was a bias in his gait which inclined him somewhat to the left of a straight line' (ll.4–5). Durbeyfield almost appears as a toddler negotiating his first steps, unconsciously meandering and nodding his head whilst 'not thinking of anything in particular'(l.7). In this state he is 'halted, and turned round' (ll.15-16) by the parson's words, calling him Sir John 'when I be plain Jack Durbeyfield' (l.24). The 'whim' (l.27) of the parson develops into an historical narrative which leaves Durbeyfield dazzled ('Daze my eyes': l.57): 'you are the lineal representative of the ancient and knightly family of the d'Urbervilles' (ll.31–3). Durbeyfield twice exclaims his incredulity before Parson Tringham's story: 'Never heard if before, sir!' and 'Ye don't say so!'; however, suddenly, the child-like Durbeyfield acquires a new identity, is named for the first time as 'Sir John', such that plain Jack Durbeyfield is transformed into the latest head of the d'Urbervilles, of whom 'there's hardly such another family in England' (l.56).

This episode is an example of what the French theorist Louis Althusser calls 'interpellation': when individuals are addressed in ways that label them (like the war poster that points a finger out at the reader and says 'Your country needs you'). Jack Durbeyfield is hailed by someone who requires that he see himself in terms of a new identity: 'you are the lineal representative' (ll.31–2), 'Yes, that's the d'Urberville nose and chin' (ll.38–9), 'Your ancestor was one of the twelve knights' (ll.39–40), 'your forefather Brian was summoned' (l.46), and 'there have been generations of Sir Johns among you' (ll.50–1). This hailing of Jack Durbeyfield is the catalyst of Tess' story, directly leading to her journey to visit the d'Urbervilles to claim kinship (and it is interesting to note that the novel's epigraph from Shakespeare's *The Two Gentleman of Verona*, though it is usually regarded to refer to Tess, actually concerns a 'name' and not a person: 'Poor wounded name! my bosom, as a bed, / Shall lodge thee': Act I, scene ii).

There are two other things I want to note about the novel's beginning: its subtitle and its structure. The subtitle asserts that Tess is 'A Pure Woman' despite transgressing a number of Victorian taboos: sex before marriage, an illegitimate child, 'living in sin' and adultery. There are several occasions in the novel when Hardy explains his reasons for this 'label', as in Chapter 39 when Angel Clare's judgement of Tess is commented upon: 'essentially this young wife of his was as deserving of the praise of King Lemuel as any other woman endowed with the same dislike of evil, her moral value having to be reckoned not by achievement but by tendency ... in considering what Tess was not, he overlooked what she was'. On the other hand, Tess is given a 'label' by Hardy and this is a point at which to consider the many ways in which Tess is fixed or stereotyped in the novel. Ellen Moers (in LaValley, 1969) has discussed Tess in terms of an 'all-purpose heroine': 'Earth goddess, modern woman, doomed bride of balladry, prostitute, Victorian daughter, unwed mother, murderess, and princess in disguise'. Moers concludes that 'Tess is a fantasy of almost pornographic dimensions, manipulated with clearly sadistic affection', and this is another way of regarding her 'fate': to epitomise the male fantasy of a madonna/whore who is both sexually available and yet 'pure'. For Hardy, the subtitle, as he argued in his 1912 preface to the novel, was 'the estimate left in a candid mind of the heroine's character – an estimate that nobody would be likely to dispute'. Yet he had found in 1891 that it was the most contentious aspect to the novel, and Moers's appraisal of Hardy's participation in the Victorian obsession with women's 'purity' made the subtitle equally contentious in the 1970s, but for entirely different reasons. For Hardy's contemporaries, Tess was not 'pure' because in the Church's terms she had 'sinned' and in society's terms she had 'fallen'; for Hardy's critics eighty years later it was the categorisation of women into 'pure' and 'unpure', and his fetishisation of Tess, that was objectionable. For Moers, Hardy's (ab)use of Tess is as great as his characters', and his insistent association of her with nature and the earth is yet another oppressive cultural stereotype.

As for the novel's structure, it is presented as a movement through seven 'phases'. *Jude the Obscure* by contrast is divided into 'parts', and so 'phases' is clearly an important word here. It suggests the phases of the moon or the cycles of nature, but could also be considered the seven ages of Tess's life, not as in the seven ages of man, but in terms of Tess's trajectory from 'Maiden' to 'martyr' in the traditional verse-structure of balladry, with its vivid, evocative scenery, clearly demarcated characters, and fateful coincidences or meetings – such as that between Durbeyfield and Parson Tringham, who appears almost like a minstrel 'on a gray mare ... humm[ing] a wandering tune'(ll.11–12).

So, Hardy's opening provides the seed from which Tess' story will grow. It is a key causal if not primal incident but does not feature the woman whose 'destiny' will unfold from it. The initial episode of the book is the impulse that leads to Tess's 'downfall' (an image of the fall of the d'Urbervilles themselves); its consequence is a series of events that moves with the inevitability of a Greek tragedy, as implied by the final paragraph of the novel, when Tess's 'fate' is described as the 'sport' of the 'President of the Immortals'. Hardy's novel is driven by a fatalistic or rational pessimism which, through its borrowings from ballads and folklore, makes Tess' story appear to follow almost ritualistically and naturally, like the phases of the moon, from Sir Pagan to Stonehenge.

Further Reading

Althusser, Louis (1971) 'Ideology and Ideological State Apparatuses' in *Lenin and Philosophy and Other Essays* (trans. Ben Brewster), London: New Left Books.

Goode, John (1988) *Thomas Hardy: The Offensive Truth*, Oxford: Basil Blackwell.

Ingham, Patricia (1989) *Thomas Hardy*, London: Harvester Wheatsheaf.

LaValley, Albert J. (ed.) (1969) *Twentieth Century Interpretations of Tess of the D'Urbervilles*, Englewood Cliffs, NJ: Prentice-Hall.

Widdowson, Peter (ed.) (1993) *Tess of the D'Urbervilles*, London: Macmillan – now Palgrave.

Henry James
The Turn of the Screw
(1898)

The story had held us, round the fire, sufficiently breathless,
but except the obvious remark that it was gruesome, as, on
Christmas eve in an old house, a strange tale should essentially
be, I remember no comment uttered till somebody happened to
say that it was the only case he had met in which such a   5
visitation has fallen on a child. The case, I may mention, was
that of an apparition in just such an old house as had gathered
us for the occasion – an appearance, of a dreadful kind, to a
little boy sleeping in the room with his mother and waking her
up in terror of it; waking her not to dissipate his dread and   10
soothe him to sleep again, but to encounter also, herself, before
she had succeeded in doing so, the same sight that had shaken
him. It was this observation that drew from Douglas – not
immediately, but later in the evening – a reply that had the
interesting consequence to which I call attention. Someone else   15
told a story not particularly effective, which I saw he was not
following. This I took for a sign that he had himself something
to produce and that we should only have to wait. We waited in
fact till two nights later; but that same evening, before we
scattered, he brought out what was in his mind.   20

'I quite agree – in regard to Griffin's ghost, or whatever it
was – that its appearing first to the little boy, at so tender an
age, adds a particular touch. But it's not the first occurrence
of its charming kind that I know to have involved a child. If
the child gives the effect another turn of the screw, what do you   25
say to *two* children – ?'

'We say, of course,' somebody exclaimed, 'that they give two
turns! Also that we want to hear about them.'

I can see Douglas there before the fire, to which he had got
up to present his back, looking down at his interlocutor with   30
his hands in his pockets. 'Nobody but me, till now, has ever

heard. It's quite too horrible.' This, naturally, was declared by
several voices to give the thing the utmost price, and our
friend, with quiet art, prepared his triumph by turning his eyes
over the rest of us and going on: 'It's beyond everything.   35
Nothing at all that I know touches it.'
    'For sheer terror?' I remember asking.
    He seemed to say it was not quite so simple as that; to be really at
a loss how to qualify it. He passed his hand over his eyes,
made a little wincing grimace. 'For dreadful – dreadfulness!'   40
    'Oh, how delicious!' cried one of the women.
    He took no notice of her; he looked at me, but as if, instead
of me, he saw what he spoke of. 'For general uncanny ugliness
and horror and pain.'
    'Well then,' I said, 'just sit right down and begin.'   45
    He turned round to the fire, gave a kick to a log, watched it
an instant. Then as he faced us again: 'I can't begin. I shall
have to send to town.' There was a unanimous groan at this,
and much reproach; after which, in his preoccupied way, he
explained. 'The story's written. It's in a locked drawer – it has   50
not been out for years. I could write to my man and enclose
the key; he could send down the packet as he finds it.' It was
to me in particular that he appeared to propound this –
appeared almost to appeal to aid not to hesitate. He had
broken a thickness of ice, the formation of many a winter; had   55
his reasons for a long silence. The others resented post-
ponement, but it was just his scruples that charmed me.
                                        (Harmondsworth: Penguin, 1969)

The transcribed manuscript that forms the core of *The Turn of the
Screw* is divided into 24 parts, like a day divided into hours.
However, this story, which constitutes the vast majority of the text, is
preceded by a framing introduction, or prologue, the beginning of
which is excerpted above. This opening creates suspense but also
introduces a number of levels between the reader and the principal
story. The tale alluded to by Douglas in the opening above will form
the main narrative of *The Turn of the Screw,* but the story will not be
an account of events that happened to him: he will read aloud to the
gathering from a manuscript sent to him by a woman, his sister's
governess, before she died 20 years ago. This introduction is therefore at several removes from the main body of the story: the first
unnamed narrator, who is telling the story to the reader, is

recounting a narrative he has heard from another character, Douglas, who says he is reading the manuscript of a third person, the unnamed governess, now long dead. The first narrator later divulges that Douglas himself is now dead and that his own narrative is *'from an exact transcript'* that he has made of the manuscript that Douglas read to him (or her – the sex of the framing narrator is not established, though most readers assume, and the story arguably implies, it is a man). Another key point to remember is that the first narrator does not return at the close of the governess's account. The framing narrative takes the form of a prologue but no epilogue, of an introduction but no conclusion; like much else in this book, it raises questions but provides no answers.

The novella itself starts at a strange moment. It opens not at the beginning of a story, but at the end of one. Immediately an absence is introduced, a first story that we will never know. However, this story concerns a boy who wakes his mother 'not to dissipate his dread' but to share in it: to 'encounter also ... the same sight that had shaken him' (ll.10–13). The adult will be unable to soothe the child, to explain away his dream, and this is also the case with *The Turn of the Screw*: it is not susceptible to reassuring logical explanation; the reader can only share in it, not explain it away. The novella's sense of suspense is also presaged in this opening sentence, which is concerned with a narrative that has 'held' its audience around the fire, the primary scene of primitive story telling, in a long snaking prose that piles clause upon clause. James delays the key word 'child', which will be at the centre of the novella, until the end of the first sentence, and indeed the story's effects are heightened throughout by James's unusual prose style, because the reader is kept in suspense until the end of each long sentence. Not that the completion of each sentence, any more than the end of the story, provides the reader with answers. James's sentence construction in this novella is not significantly different from that which he uses elsewhere, but it is well-suited to a story steeped in doubts and uncertainties. In this opening there are many expressions that complement the suggestiveness of the narrative: *turns* of phrase like the double-conjunction 'but except' (l.2), unexplained details like 'Griffin's ghost, or whatever it was' (l.21), and names such as 'Griffin' (l.21: a griffin is a fabulous beast with the head and wings of an eagle and the body of a lion). There are also grammatical features that add to the suspense, as well as unusual punctuation ' – ?' (l. 26) and snaking sentences (just the first two occupy twelve lines) that seem to suggest a maze in which the reader appears to be gaining more information, as clause is piled upon clause (there are 11 in the second sentence), but is in fact being forced to continue and stop, to progress and pause, in a series of jolting false starts that leave him or her breathless and frustrated. The reader is left wondering what the narrator is actually getting at or trying to say, and is thus held in suspense just as the first story, which is unknown to the reader, 'had held us, round the fire' (l.1). In this way, the style matches the unsolved puzzles of the tale itself: questions concerning the identity of Douglas, and his relation to the governess, the inquiry into Miles's death, the mystery surrounding the Master, let alone what Quint and Jessel might have done to the children, remain without answers.

The adjectives used to describe the narratives recounted to the gathering at the start of *The Turn of the Screw* accentuate the two most common kinds of response to ghost stories, which often, as here, go hand in hand. Thus, they are seen as 'charming' (l.24) and 'delicious' (l.41), but at the same time they are 'dreadful' (l.40) and 'horrible' (l.32). This awful fascination for the macabre epitomises a feeling of ambivalence: a simultaneous attraction and repulsion. Such a dual response is also expressed by the word 'uncanny' (l.43), which describes something whose identity, nature or familiarity is undecided in a way that is perturbing. An uncanny likeness is one which appears strangely familiar. Also anything which seems to question rigidly divided categories can be called uncanny, as when we are in doubt whether someone is male or female, or whether we have visited a place before, or, in the case of ghost stories, whether someone is alive or not, or even whether they are human or not (for a fuller discussion of the uncanny, especially its use by Freud, see Further Reading below). In James's tale this ambivalence works at the level of the story, particularly with regard to the division between the natural and the supernatural, but also at the level of the narration. As generations of critics have found, it is impossible to decide conclusively what actually happens: whether the governess' story involves ghosts or hallucinations and whether she is deceived or not. While her sincerity is not in doubt, her reliability is always open to question. If she is correct in thinking that she has seen ghosts, her testimony lacks corroboration from those around her and is undermined by the inconsistencies of her own account of events; but if she has been a victim of hallucinations or delusions, then some aspects, such as her description of the first apparition, supposedly the ghost of a man she has never seen, are uncanny in their accuracy.

The ambiguity of much of the dialogue in the story, combined with the indeterminacy of the narrative, places the reader in a position where single interpretations border on the psychiatric definition of delusion: 'a belief held in the face of evidence to the contrary, that is resistant to reason'. While the governess's story does not add up, neither can the reader's interpretation because it must also be partial, must foreground certain details of the story while putting others in the background: a comment less on the inconsistencies of the governess's narrative than on the act of interpretation itself which, unless it is merely to repeat the text, must highlight particular aspects for special emphasis while marginalising others. In this way, as in others, the difficulties of reading connected with *The Turn of the Screw* ultimately point to the fundamental problem of interpretation: that the attribution of 'meaning' is a process of summarising and selecting.

For example, to corroborate the interpretation that the governess is deluded, a reader could draw attention to the following phrase from the opening pages: 'he looked at me, but as if, instead of me, he saw what he spoke of' (ll.42–3). If this is taken as a significant line it could be said that, in a tale littered with words like 'seemed', appeared' and 'imagined', the ghosts 'seen' by the governess are similarly a case of her not seeing what is there but what she speaks of in her narrative. Similarly, the reference to Douglas having 'brought out what was in his mind' appears to work equally well as a description of hallucination. Perhaps it should also not be overlooked that Douglas introduces his story 'with quiet art' (l.34).

Additionally, like many other narratives based on 'oral stories', *The Turn of the Screw* has a layering of narration: the main story, contained in the packet that Douglas has to send for, is read out loud to a hushed gathering around the hearth. This adds to the suspense but also calls upon us to believe the story, to witness the first narrator's simultaneous incredulity *and* belief in what is being told. Perhaps most significantly, the main narrative of the book is traced in these opening scenes to a written text, unread for many years, deposited 'in a locked drawer' (l.50). The retelling of the story, therefore, is repeatedly deferred, covered over, as though with 'a thickness of ice' (l.55), by a series of obscurities and silences (for example, l.56). And, the written text, crucially, is not that of its owner, Douglas; rather it is, we are told a couple of paragraphs after the opening quoted above, '"in old faded ink and in the most beautiful hand." He hung fire again. "A woman's. She has been dead these twenty years. She sent me the pages in question before she died."' Douglas actually has to write, with 'the key' (l.52), to 'his man' so that the manuscript may be sent, and the manuscript then is received by him on the third day of the action. Interestingly, the narrator points out that Douglas only begins to read it to 'the hushed little circle' on the night of the fourth. There is a pervading sense, in other words, of a sequence of narrative 'suspensions' or 'delays'. The sense of the story's delay and deferral is further emphasised by two more elements introduced before the governess's narrative itself begins: first, the initial narrator's revelation that he is re-telling the story after Douglas's death. The narrative we actually read, therefore, is supposed to be a transcript of Douglas's reading of the governess's faded manuscript. Second, the fact that Douglas's reading of the manuscript is considered, apparently, to warrant a prologue. Which is to say, the narrative apparently cannot stand on its own, not least because it is later stressed that 'the written statement took up the tale at a point after it had, in a manner, begun'.

Lastly, it it worth noting that the title of the novella is mentioned on the opening page, but nowhere else in the book. It is chosen by the framing 'Jamesian' narrator who takes it from Douglas's early remark. Ostensibly, its meaning applies to the introduction of a child as a first witness to ghosts in Griffin's tale (1.22). Douglas's reading of the governess' story will produce another turn by involving two children. Yet, the reader may well feel differently about the meaning of this expression having read the book, after which it seems more to apply to the mounting hysteria, or tightening dread, of the governess' story, in which each chapter adds a further twist to the reader's impression of what has gone before. Ultimately, with regard to interpretation the story is indeed 'beyond everything' (1.35).

Further Reading

Bennett, Andrew and Royle, Nicholas (1999) 'The Uncanny' in *An Introduction to Literature, Criticism and Theory* (2nd edn), Hemel Hempstead: Prentice-Hall.

Cornwell, Neil and Malone, Maggie (eds) (1998) *The Turn of the Screw and What Maisie Knew*, London: Macmillan – now Palgrave.

Felman, Shoshana (1982) 'Turning the Screw of Interpretation' in *Literature and Psychoanalysis: the question of reading: otherwise* (ed. S. Felman), Baltimore, MD: Johns Hopkins University Press: 94–207.

Freud, Sigmund (1985) 'The Uncanny' (1919) in *Pelican Freud Library*, vol. 14 (trans. James Strachey) Harmondsworth: Penguin.

Lustig, T.J. (1994) *Henry James and the Ghostly*, Cambridge: Cambridge University Press.

Chapter

Joseph Conrad
Heart of Darkness
(1899–1902)

11

The *Nellie*, a cruising yawl, swung to her anchor without a
flutter of the sails, and was at rest. The flood had made, the
wind was nearly calm, and being bound down the river, the
only thing for it was to come to and wait for the turn of the
tide.   5

The sea-reach of the Thames stretched before us like the
beginning of an interminable waterway. In the offing the sea
and the sky were welded together without a joint, and in the
luminous space the tanned sails of the barges drifting up with
the tide seemed to stand still in red clusters of canvas sharply   10
peaked, with gleams of varnished sprits. A haze rested on the
low shores that ran out to sea in vanishing flatness. The air
was dark above Gravesend, and farther back still seemed
condensed into a mournful gloom, brooding motionless over
the biggest, and the greatest, town on earth.   15

The Director of Companies was our captain and our host.
We four affectionately watched his back as he stood in the
bows looking to seaward. On the whole river there was nothing
that looked half so nautical. He resembled a pilot, which to a
seaman is trustworthiness personified. It was difficult to realise   20
his work was not out there in the luminous estuary, but
behind him, within the brooding gloom.

Between us there was, as I have already said somewhere,
the bond of the sea. Besides holding our hearts together
through long periods of separation, it had the effect of making   25
us tolerant of each other's yarns – and even convictions. The
Lawyer – the best of old fellows – had, because of his many
years and many virtues, the only cushion on deck, and was
lying on the only rug. The Accountant had brought out
already a box of dominoes, and was toying architecturally with   30
the bones. Marlow sat cross-legged right aft, leaning against

the mizzen-mast. He had sunken cheeks, a yellow complexion,
a straight back, an ascetic aspect, and, with his arms dropped,
the palms of hands outwards, resembled an idol. The Director, satisfied the anchor had good hold, made his way aft and   35
sat down amongst us. We exchanged a few words lazily.
Afterwards there was silence on board the yacht. For some
reason or other we did not begin that game of dominoes. We
felt meditative, and fit for nothing but placid staring. The day
was ending in a serenity of still and exquisite brilliance. The   40
water shone pacifically; the sky, without a speck, was a benign
immensity of unstained light; the very mist on the Essex
marshes was like a gauzy, and radiant fabric, hung from the
wooded rises inland, and draping the low shores in diaphanous
folds. Only the gloom to the west, brooding over the upper   45
reaches, became more sombre every minute, as if angered by
the approach of the sun.

   And at last, in its curved and imperceptible fall, the sun
sank low, and from glowing white changed to a dull red
without rays and without heat, as if about to go out suddenly,   50
stricken to death by the touch of that gloom brooding over a
crowd of men.

(Harmondsworth: Penguin, 1995)

Conrad's novella is an inscrutable play of language: words are repeated and reinflected throughout the text in a way that leaves the reader unsure of their final meanings. Certain words and phrases are reiterated even in this opening section, such as the 'brooding gloom' (ll.14, 22, 45 and 51) which is opposed to the 'luminous' (ll.9 and 21) river. Thus the major opposition, between the 'light' (associated with Europe) and the 'dark' (linked with Africa) is established from the outset. The title itself is fundamentally ambiguous and has been the subject of numerous interpretations, suggesting it refers to Africa, Europe, the Belgian Empire, colonialism, the unconscious, or to the human heart. The number of words and phrases which refer to either 'dark' or 'light' imagery in just this opening 50 lines is notably high, and each reference refines the metaphorical importance attaching to the two terms, leaving expressions like 'brilliance', 'radiant fabric' and 'immensity of unstained light' (ll.40–3) without the straight-forward positive associations they would usually have.

   If we consider more fully this indeterminacy, it is important that Conrad's first narrator, who soon hands over to the main narrator,

Marlow, makes reference early on to the 'haze' resting upon the shore (l.11), which is reintroduced later as the 'mist on the Essex marshes' (l.42). This presages one of the most famous passages in all of Conrad's fiction, when the narrator says of Marlow a few pages later that 'to him the meaning of an episode was not inside like a kernel but outside, enveloping the tale which brought it out only as a glow brings out a haze, in the likeness of one of these misty halos that sometimes are made visible by the spectral illumination of moonshine' (p.18). The implication is that the 'meaning' of *Heart of Darkness* will be found in its enigmas, conjectures, and even mysteries – in the complexities of language and the ways in which nebulous desires surround human behaviour.

The book's chief character and principal narrator, the 'cross-legged' Marlow (l.31), is introduced as resembling 'an idol' (l.34). This also initiates a chain of connections in the story, in which idol worship is used by Conrad to show the falsity and greed of the colonial project. I will give three instances of this motif: first, Conrad creates Kurtz as a figure of worship for all those around him, who are in awe, including Marlow; second, colonialism is also made into an idol, as when we are told later that, 'What redeems [the conquest of the earth] is the idea only ... something you can set up, and bow down before, and offer a sacrifice to'; third, Marlow, we are later informed twice by the framing narrator, sits in 'the pose of a [meditating] Buddha'. These parallels are there to make the reader connect characters and events across the narrative, to see that the corrupt Kurtz is not unique, but a double for Marlow, and for most other Europeans confronted with the possibility of wealth and power. This aspect is anticipated in the opening by the accountant 'toying architecturally with the bones' (ll.30–1), suggesting the exploitation of the Africans later in the story and also the trade in ivory, from which the dominoes are made. Overall, the book's narrative works through a number of such parallels. For example, there is an early discussion of the Roman colonisation of Britain that again tries to link Africans and Europeans through an analogy with Europe's ancestors: London also 'has been one of the dark places of the earth' we are told by Marlow in his first utterance.

Importantly, in terms of sailors' yarns but also pre-literate culture, Conrad uses the conventions of oral storytelling. The novella begins with a group sitting in semi-darkness listening to each other take turns to tell stories to pass the time as they wait for the tide to turn. Conrad does this to mimic the archetypal scene of a story told around the village or hunters' fire at night. Also, on board the *Nellie*

Conrad uses a cast of businessmen known only as the Accountant, the Lawyer and the Director to emphasise that colonialism in Africa has become a business, a commercial concern, and no longer the prerogative of entrepreneurial explorers and missionaries such as David Livingstone.

The opening creates a sense of enormous calm, as well as sinister foreboding: on the one hand there are words like 'serenity', 'still', 'pacifically', 'calm', 'unruffled', 'motionless', 'placid' and 'silence'; on the other 'mournful', 'gloom', 'brooding' and 'sombre'. This is appropriate to the way that the novel develops from this serene opening to Kurtz's final pronouncement of 'the horror', and it shows the way in which for Conrad the equanimity with which colonialism was received in Europe stood alongside the barbarism of the Europeans in Africa. Another set of images in the novel is initiated at the opening, and that is to do with clothing, covering and drapery, most obviously in this image: 'the very mist on the Essex marshes was like a gauzy, and radiant fabric, hung from the wooded rises inland, and draping the low shores in diaphanous folds' (ll.42–5). If we take one word from this sentence, such as 'draping', we can see the way in which the novella repeats its terms, which thus accumulate significances. For example, each time the figure of a woman appears in the novella, she is associated with this first image: Kurtz's sketch in oils depicts a figure 'draped and blindfolded', then the African woman on the shore is 'draped in striped and fringed cloths', while at the book's end the Intended meets Marlow amid 'draped columns'. Drapery is for Conrad an image of clothing, but also one of deception and covering, like the magnificent eloquence with which Kurtz is cloaked to hide his own rapacious desires, or 'heart of darkness', and the rhetoric used to conceal the way that the colonialists themselves 'go at it blind', as if blindfolded.

Conrad's story is deliberately narrated as a journey into the self, a psychological self-discovery. Marlow, the civilised white man, journeys into the heart of the 'dark' continent and confronts there a savage white man, Kurtz – his double. For Conrad, the story was reminding his Victorian readers of a message similar to Freud's at the same time: that at the core of every civilised individual are violent desires (at the dark heart). Many phrases in Conrad's book point us towards this conclusion, such as when we are told that 'The mind of man is capable of anything.' However, for a critic such as Frantz Fanon in *Black Skin, White Masks*, it is the unequal power relations between coloniser and colonised that create the structural relation of mutual degradation. Fanon drew his insights from his work in

Algerian psychiatric hospitals, where he found that the colonial situation turned the French into torturers and the Algerians into dehumanised sufferers: a Manichean struggle between light and dark, good and evil, reflected throughout in the very language of Conrad's novella. The associations which accrete around the words 'dark' and 'light' in *Heart of Darkness* leave the terms themselves empty and hollow, signifiers which have slipped from signified to signified so often they can no longer serve as metaphors for anything but each other. And this is the end of the novella's journey, yet it has arrived here only from an assumption of superiority, of European enlightenment over dark African otherness. Once Marlow returns to Brussels at the end of the book he will begin to readjust: he still knows the animality that is in his heart but he also knows that only 'primitive' places like Africa will release that recidivistic darkness which European civilisation has hidden away behind institutionalised restraints. The colonial connection between Britain and Africa is there at the start in Conrad's description of the Thames, which 'stretched before us like the beginning of an interminable waterway' (ll.6–7), an image repeated in the final sentence of the book to remind the reader that it is only water that separates, and so links, Europe and Africa.

It is worth adding in conclusion that the opening to *Heart of Darkness* is literally a meditation on the sun setting on the capital of the British Empire, over the 'biggest ... greatest, town on earth' (l.15). The sun has 's[u]nk low' and is 'about to go out suddenly, stricken to death by the touch of that gloom brooding over a crowd of men' (ll.50–2), which is Conrad's metaphor for the poison introduced by the greed and inefficiency of the colonial enterprise: the main theme of the book, for which the darkness of the title is a symbol. Colonialism's ideal, the idea at the back of it, is to spread enlightenment just as the sun spreads its radiance across the world, but the truth is that the colonial enterprise has turned to rapacity, greed and blood-letting: has 'from glowing white changed to a dull red without rays and without heat' (ll.49–50).

Further Reading

Burden, Robert (1991) *Heart of Darkness*, London: Macmillan – now Palgrave.
Fanon, Frantz (1986) *Black Skins, White Masks* (trans. Charles Lam Markham), London: Pluto.
Roberts, Andrew Michael (ed.) (1998) *Joseph Conrad*, Harlow: Longman.
Youngs, Tim (1994) *Travellers in Africa*, Manchester: Manchester University Press.

12

Ford Madox Ford
The Good Soldier
(1915)

This is the saddest story I have ever heard. We had known
the Ashburnhams for nine seasons of the town of Nauheim
with an extreme intimacy – or, rather, with an acquaintance as loose and easy and yet as close as a good glove's
with your hand. My wife and I knew Captain and Mrs   5
Ashburnham as well as it is possible to know anybody,
and yet, in another sense, we knew nothing at all about
them. This is, I believe, a state of things only possible with
English people of whom, till today, when I sit down to
puzzle out what I know of this sad affair, I knew nothing   10
whatever. Six months ago I had never been to England,
and, certainly, I had never sounded the depths of an English
heart. I had known the shallows.

I don't mean to say that we were not acquainted with
many English people. Living, as we perforce lived, in   15
Europe, and being, as we perforce were, leisured Americans, which is as much as to say that we were un-American,
we were thrown very much into the society of the nicer
English. Paris, you see, was our home. Somewhere between
Nice and Bordighera provided yearly winter quarters for   20
us, and Nauheim always received us from July to Septem-
ber. You will gather from this statement that one of us had,
as the saying is, a 'heart', and, from the statement that my
wife is dead, that she was the sufferer.

Captain Ashburnham also had a heart. But, whereas a   25
yearly month or so at Nauheim tuned him up to exactly the
right pitch for the rest of the twelvemonth, the two months
or so were only just enough to keep poor Florence alive
from year to year. The reason for his heart was, approximately, polo, or too much hard sportsmanship in his youth.   30
The reason for poor Florence's broken years was a storm at

sea upon our first crossing to Europe, and the immediate
reasons for our imprisonment in that continent were doctor's orders. They said that even the short Channel crossing
might well kill the poor thing.   35

When we all first met, Captain Ashburnham, home on
sick leave from an India to which he was never to return,
was thirty-three; Mrs Ashburnham – Leonora – was thirty-
one. I was thirty-six and poor Florence thirty. Thus today
Florence would have been thirty-nine and Captain Ash-   40
burnham forty-two; whereas I am forty-five and Leonora
forty. You will perceive, therefore, that our friendship has
been a young-middle-aged affair, since we were all of us of
quite quiet dispositions, the Ashburnhams being more particularly what in England it is the custom to call 'quite   45
good people'.

They were descended, as you will probably expect, from
the Ashburnham who accompanied Charles I to the scaffold,
and, as you must also expect with this class of English
people, you would never have noticed it. Mrs Ashburnham   50
was a Powys; Florence was a Hurlbird of Stamford, Connecticut, where, as you know, they are more old-fashioned
than even the inhabitants of Cranford, England, could have
been. I myself am a Dowell of Philadelphia, Pa., where, it
is historically true, there are more old English families   55
than you would find in any six English counties taken together.

(Harmondsworth: Penguin, 1972)

Ford's book opens with one of the most striking but also enigmatic
statements in English literature. The narrator, John Dowell, asserts
that this is 'the saddest story' (Ford's preferred title for the novel) he
has ever *heard*. However, the story he recounts is one in which he has
participated, not one he has simply heard. The novel's irony and
pathos rests on the fact that Dowell has not understood or even
realised the truth of what has happened to him (with 'English people
of whom, till today ... I knew nothing whatever': ll.9–11). He has
'heard' the story only in the sense that someone else has told him
what has 'really been going on'. Dowell's misleading narratorial
style, which will characterise the twists and turns of the rest of the
book, is also present on this first page when he mentions his wife's
death (ll.22–4), which in fact had nothing to do with her heart, but

was by suicide (p.115). He addresses the reader directly (for example, 'As you will probably expect': l.47) and qualifies his opinions (for example, 'This is, I believe, a state of things': l.8) in a conversational manner that is always likely to undermine itself (for example, 'I don't mean to say that': l.14).

Borrowing from nineteenth-century fiction, Dowell attempts to be a detached narrator who makes his hero, Edward Ashburnham, into the 'good soldier' of the title: polo-player (l.30), aristocrat (ll.47–9), imperialist (l.37) and heart-sufferer. However, Ford satirises this kind of novelistic adoration, glorifying supposedly heroic individuals, by making Dowell's idol have a longterm affair with Dowell's wife (the repeated word 'affair' on line 10 and line 43 has greater resonance for this reason). The four main characters are introduced at the end of this opening: Captain Edward Ashburnham, descended 'from the Ashburnham who accompanied Charles I to the scaffold' (an allusion to Edward's suicide by slitting his throat); his wife, Leonora, from whom Dowell thinks he has learned much of the truth about the last nine years; Dowell, a Philadelphian Quaker; and his wife Florence, from an old-fashioned Connecticut family and referred to repeatedly by Dowell as 'poor' (ll.31, 35, 39) because of her putative heart condition. The four have met each summer for nine years at the town of Nauheim, for the rest cures needed by Florence, supposedly, and Edward.

On one level, the book concerns oppositions between public and private worlds. The public world for the story's central quartet revolves around the upper-class, 'leisured' (l.16), Edwardian land-owning elite which purports to uphold Victorian moral standards and propriety. The characters lead idle lives, with little employment, no family, and anachronistic social and economic roles alongside the rising commercial classes. Dowell himself, having nothing better to do, even spends his time counting his own footsteps. Above all, with these characters, it is the public façade that matters: Dowell says they have a dread of scenes, scandals, publicity or open confrontations (p.61).

In *The Good Soldier*, the one character who has been taken in by the veneer of the old polished world of manners, the hypocrisy of European gentility, is the narrator. Dowell is from America, the 'new world', but he is the prime exponent of an old *European* social mythology and he embodies the beliefs of Victorian morality. Both he and Florence are more English than the English:

Florence was a Hurlbird of Stamford, Connecticut, where, as you know, they are more old-fashioned than even the inhabitants of Cranford, England, could have been. I myself am a Dowell of Philadelphia, Pa., where, it is historically true, there are more old English families than you would find in any six English counties together. (ll.51–7)

Dowell says: 'I will vouch for the cleanliness of my thoughts and the absolute chastity of my life' (p.18). He admires 'manly' virtue, is condescending and dismissive of his black servant and gently patronising to all women. Consequently, he also believes his wife Florence to be the ideal Victorian woman: delicate, virtuous, and in need of protection from all excitement because of the strain this would put on her heart (ll.22–4). The colloquialism 'had a heart' (ll.22–3 and 25) is used ironically of Edward and Florence to indicate both the passion between them and the seeming heartlessness of their adulteries. There is also a typical ambiguity in this last sentence of the second paragraph: 'You will gather from this statement that one of us had, as the saying is, a "heart", and, from the statement that my wife is dead, that she was the sufferer.' The superficial meaning is clearly that Florence suffered from a weak heart; but this is something Dowell now knows to be untrue. The statement therefore works to illustrate one way in which appearances can be deceiving. The reader 'will gather' incorrectly, as Dowell has repeatedly done. It also allows different understandings of the sentence: Florence had a 'heart', but in the sense of one which could 'break' not malfunction, or perhaps the reader will alternatively come to feel that it was Dowell who was the one who had 'a heart', not the deceiving Florence.

Through his narrative, Dowell tries to come to terms with events but soon finds that the modern world will not fit any system, such that he slips repeatedly into saying to the reader 'I don't know' or 'you sort it out' (Dowell's conversational, insecure style is present in this opening section in the phrase addressed to the reader, 'you see' (l.19), and in his qualification, 'with an extreme intimacy – or, rather with an acquaintanceship' (ll.3–4), repeated in the following sentence's equivocation: 'and yet, in another sense' (l.7)). Ford here expresses a shift from nineteenth-century certainty to modernist disorientation through Dowell's increasingly inept narration. Dowell tries to tell the story with the competency and omniscience of a third-person narrator, but he is forced to admit his limitations, his incomplete knowledge. To put this in a historical context, by 1913, when Ford began writing the novel, several theories had already prompted a shift away from Victorian confidence towards modernist uncertainty. After the assaults on religion of Marxist and Darwinian beliefs, Nietzsche had openly denied the existence of God and the possibility of absolute truth. Alongside the developing impact of Freud's theories of psychoanalysis, Einstein's 1905 theory of relativity had gained a hold on many European intellectuals. Consequently, this left a residual belief in the individual: it was the observer on whom concentration should be focused, not the event. There is as a result no authority in the novel, mimicking the absence of certainty in the larger world. Dowell makes mistakes about dates and names, changes his mind, contradicts himself, forgets things, gets events in the wrong order, and so on; he is an unreliable narrator.

The novel is subtitled 'a tale of passion' and many critics have observed that the book is in several respects centred on the struggle between convention and passion. Usually the focus is on the way that passions differentiate people while conventions encourage homogeneity. In this way, Dowell is caught between appearances and revelations. Also, as any dictionary would record, there are at least three readings of this 'passion'. First, sexual passion, which Dowell calls 'madnesses', in true Victorian style. Second, 'the suffering of pain', as in Christ's passion or a passion play, which for Ford, as a Catholic, is probably the most important meaning of the word because 'passion' in this sense could apply to any character in the novel, where words such as 'hell', 'agony', and 'pain' are commonplace (there is a foretaste of this in the opening when Dowell refers to 'our imprisonment' in Europe: (1.33). Third, 'passivity', which etymologically means 'capable of suffering', and which clearly relates to Dowell, who is passive before Florence's desires and deceptions on the one hand and the conventions of the English on the other (Dowell is what his name literally means: a dowel is a piece of wood used to fasten pieces together and to hang things from; the story hangs off Dowell, who connects the narrative pieces together, but he is himself wooden and in many ways fixed).

Dowell is a compelling figure and critical views on him vary enormously: is he misled or disoriented by his environment? Is he a strong-principled Quaker who naively attempts to apply his own strict codes to the other characters? Is he repressed and unbalanced? Is he a neurotic who is emotionally-retarded and impotent? Should he be seen primarily in existentialist terms (Dowell is bewildered in the agony of a universe without God, morality or reason), or is he a latent homosexual, in love with Edward but unable to come to terms with his feelings? Or, finally, is he a symptom of his environment, of the callous, idle, upper classes who were leading Europe to war?

Ford called himself an 'impressionist' writer and the word 'impression' itself recurs throughout the book. He is interested at all points in the impression that incidents create on people rather than 'facts' or 'truth'. This is a technique Ford derived from the impressionist painters. Just as those artists believed in changing light to alter the object observed, Ford makes Dowell return to the same situations with new light to shed on them (sounding as though he is describing a pointilliste painting, Dowell at one point also says events are to him like 'spots of colour on a canvas'). Ford makes it clear that no one else would tell the story the way that Dowell does. For example, Dowell is distinctive in the way that he often provides a list of details and then ends with a statement that underlines what has gone before, like 'poor devil' or 'that's the way it was with us', or, in this section, 'I had known the shallows' (l.13). Above all, the book is narrated out of Dowell's personal impressions, which are seen from his unique perspective at any one moment.

Lastly, the Ashburnhams are here called 'quite good people' (ll.45–6) but, like *Heart of Darkness*, the main terms of *The Good Soldier* are not to be taken at face value. Dowell describes the world of the two couples as 'a prison full of screaming hysterics' (p.14) and concludes of the other charaters: 'I think that it would have been better in the eyes of God if they had all attempted to gouge out each other's eyes with carving knives. But they were "good people"' (p.223). These are the good people whose feudal morality and anachronistic code of honour will shortly send millions to gouge each other with bayonets. It is therefore from at least one angle a further irony that the novel's subtitle is *Beati Immaculati* (blessed are the pure), an expression which has to be analysed for its plurality of meanings, like the subtitle 'A Pure Woman' to Hardy's *Tess of the D'Urbervilles*, and in the same multiple ways as the novel's other keywords, such as 'good' and 'passion'. Ultimately, one of the principal messages of *The Good Soldier* seems to be that words, like people, do not necessarily mean what they appear to mean.

Further Reading

Childs, Peter (2000) *Modernism*, London: Routledge.
Poole, Roger (1990) 'The Real Plot Line of Ford Madox Ford's *The Good Soldier*: an essay in applied deconstruction', *Textual Practice*, 4:3 (Winter).

Ford, Ford Madox (1995) *The Good Soldier*, ed. by Martin Stannard, Norton Critical Edition), New York: Norton.

Swinden, Patrick (1973) *Unofficial Selves: Character in the Novel from Dickens to the Present Day*, London: Macmillan – now Palgrave.

James Joyce
A Portrait of the Artist as
a Young Man *(1916)*

Once upon a time and a very good time it was there was
a moocow coming down along the road and this moocow
that was coming down along the road met a nicens little
boy named baby tuckoo....

His father told him that story: his father looked at him   5
through a glass: he had a hairy face.

He was baby tuckoo. The moocow came down the
road where Betty Byrne lived: she sold lemon platt.

O, the wild rose blossoms
On the little green place.   10

He sang that song. That was his song.

O, the green wothe botheth.

When you wet the bed first it is warm and then it gets cold.
His mother put on the oilsheet. That had the queer smell.

His mother had a nicer smell than his father. She played   15
on the piano the sailor's hornpipe for him to dance. He
danced:

Tralala lala
Tralala tralaladdy
Tralala lala   20
Tralala lala.

Uncle Charles and Dante clapped. They were older
than his father and mother but Uncle Charles was older
than Dante.

Dante had two brushes in her press. The brush with   25
the maroon velvet back was for Michael Davitt and the

brush with the green velvet back was for Parnell. Dante
gave him a cachou every time he brought her a piece of
tissue paper.

The Vances lived in number seven. They had a different   30
father and mother. They were Eileen's father and mother.
When they were grown up he was going to marry Eileen.
He hid under the table. His mother said:

– O, Stephen will apologise. –

Dante said: 35

– O, if not, eagles will come and pull out his eyes. –

Pull out his eyes,
Apologise,
Apologise,
Pull out his eyes.   40

Apologise,
Pull out his eyes,
Pull out his eyes,
Apologise.

*   *   *

The wide playgrounds were swarming with boys. All   45
were shouting and the prefects urged them on with strong
cries. The evening air was pale and chilly and after every
charge and thud of the footballers the greasy leather orb
flew like a heavy bird through the grey light. He kept on
the fringe of his line, out of sight of his prefect, out of the 50
reach of the rude feet, feigning to run now and then. He
felt his body small and weak amid the throng of players
and his eyes were weak and watery. Rody Kickham was
not like that: he would be captain of the third line all
the fellows said.   55

Rody Kickham was a decent fellow but Nasty Roche
was a stink. Rody Kickham had greaves in his number
and a hamper in the refectory. Nasty Roche had big
hands. He called the Friday pudding dog-in-the-basket.
And one day he had asked: 60
    – What is your name?
Stephen had answered: Stephen Dedalus.

(Harmondsworth: Penguin, 1992)

Joyce's first novel, following the publication of the short story collection *Dubliners* in 1914, was published in the year of the Easter Rising, 1916, when Irish Independence was declared, temporarily, by nationalists who saw their opportunity for liberation while Britain was fighting the Great War. Joyce seemed only to publish his novels in momentous years: *Ulysses* appeared in 1922, the year Ireland became independent, and *Finnegan's Wake* was published in the year the Second World War started.

A Portrait of the Artist as a Young Man covers the years 1883–1903 and is largely autobiographical. The long title is itself quite complex. It identifies three people: the painter, the sitter, and the young man portrayed. But in this case they are all the same person. The effect is to create a triangular relation between the artist's three-in-one Trinity of selves.

Portrait-painter (Artist 1)

Portrait-subject (Artist 2   **Portrait-object (Artist 3**
[in present])   **[in past])**

The book is interested in all these three figures (which are also father, son, and Holy Ghost) and in the relationship between these aspects to Stephen Dedalus, Joyce's surrogate, as portraitist, portrayed and portrait. The third-person narrator, who often writes using Stephen's language, appears as the portrait painter, and he writes systematically about the social, religious, political and sexual development of a boy up to his university years, but his interest will be in his protagonist's growth into an artist. Joyce is therefore deeply concerned with technical uses of language, the tool of the novelist, and the narrator has at times an extremely close relationship to the central character, which is why the book starts with the first example of a story that a child is likely to encounter: a simple tale beginning 'Once upon a time'. Joyce's novel at all points uses language appropriate to Stephen's age. These opening paragraphs take the reader from Stephen's earliest memories through to his first days at Clongowes school.

Joyce begins the novel with a fairy-tale opening to suggest a child's first encounter with narrative: that is to say, the story Stephen hears is written by Joyce with no punctuation, to convey that it is an oral narrative, heard by a child with no knowledge of language in its written form. The tale is told by an indulgent parent, with comical asides ('and a very good time it was': l.1) and with repetitions ('there was a moocow coming down along the road and this moocow that was coming down along the road': l.2). These may indicate that his father, Simon, is drunk, which would be one reason why he does not smell as nice as Stephen's mother (l.15) and would also explain the 'glass' in line 6 that he looks at Stephen through (there are other explanations, such as a reading glass or a monocle, but the story is told and not *read* to Stephen). The line 'through a glass', in this context of children's language and a child and a man face-to-face, inevitably also echoes I Corinthians 13:11: 'When I was a child I spake as a child, I understood as a child, I thought as a child: but when I became a man, I put away childish things. For now we see through a glass, darkly; but then face to face.'

The third paragraph tells us that Stephen is 'baby tuckoo' (l.7), the 'nicens' little boy of his father's story. 'Tuckoo' is presumably a perversion of cuckoo and so suggests the herald of spring, a child in the wrong nest/home, and flight. These last two meanings are crucial to the novel (and to *Ulysses* where Stephen, in the role of Homer's Telemachus, goes in quest of a father), which builds up to Stephen's flight from Ireland and his search for his spiritual father: both of which are symbolised in his surname. Stephen at times accepts but then later in the novel rejects both Simon as father and God as Father, but at the novel's conclusion he places his faith in the paternal figure suggested by his surname, the last word of this extract. Daedalus was the great Cretan artificer of Greek mythology, who built the labyrinth, in which dwelt the Minotaur, and later escaped from Crete with his son Icarus by making wings for them both. The name suggests that Stephen will also be a great artist; hence the novel's final sentence: 'Old father, old artificer, stand me now and ever in good stead.' Stephen writes this in his diary as he prepares to fly Ireland's nets, to move to the Continent and, as he famously writes in the penultimate paragraph of the book, 'to forge in the smithy of my soul the uncreated conscience of my race'. In line with this, the novel's epigraph is taken from Ovid's discussion of Daedalus in his *Metamorphoses*, '*Et ignotas animum dimittit in artes*' ('he abandoned his mind to obscure arts').

The songs that follow in lines 9–20 are again reminders of Stephen's first attempts to master language as well as his first experiences of the pleasure of narratives and sounds, particularly the rhythmical, musical qualities of words ('Tralala lala'). By the end of the songs Joyce has subtly taken us through a journey of the senses. Stephen's first memories involve hearing ('his father told him that story': 1.5), then sight ('his father ... he had a hairy face': 1.5–6), followed by taste (Betty Byrne's 'lemon platt': 1.8), touch ('when you wet the bed first it is warm then it gets cold': 1.13), and finally smell (the oilsheet 'had the queer smell': 1.14). Each one has been introduced to indicate Stephen's developing involvement in and understanding of the world. Similarly, the first real people introduced in the story are the boy's father and mother, followed by his uncle and aunt, Charles and Dante. The relatives are accorded a place in Stephen's mind according to the hierarchy used by most children, which is age: 'They were older than his father and mother but Uncle Charles was older than Dante' (ll.21–3).

The theme of politics is introduced by Dante's brushes: one for the Protestant Charles Stewart Parnell and one for the Catholic Michael Davitt. Parnell was Joyce's political hero: with Davitt he had founded the Land League in 1879, he became the leader of 61 Home Rule League members elected to Parliament in 1880, and he pressed unceasingly for Irish Independence over the following decade. The wrangling later in Chapter 1 (pp.29–39), between Dante, a loyal devotee of the Church, and Stephen's father, a supporter of Parnell, plays out Joyce's own bitter feelings about Parnell's betrayal by the priests and by their followers in Ireland. Dante's green brush also links to the earlier song, the only other time colour has been mentioned ('green place', l. 10 and 'the green wothe botheth', l. 12), to suggest the political import of the novel by beginning with Ireland's national colour.

Expanding from the small circle of relatives who congregate in his house, Stephen next thinks of the people who are the Dedalus' next door neighbours, the Vances. In Stephen's young mind everyone is a member of a family, and so the Vances are identified by their 'different' (they are Protestant) father and mother, and by Eileen, the girl who will supposedly become a mother to Stephen's role as father when they grow up (1.32). The next sentence implies that Stephen wishes to take his place in the adult world by marrying Eileen. Alternatively, it suggests that the fantasy of a future marriage is more his parents' idea than his own, something he tries to hide from under the table, as he will later try to escape the nets of religion, family and nation:

> I will not serve that in which I no longer believe, whether it call itself my home, my fatherland, or my church: and I will try to express myself in some mode of life or art as freely as I can and as wholly as I can, using for my defence the only arms I allow myself to use – silence, exile, and cunning. (p.269)

Stephen's defiant assertion 'I will not serve', which was also Lucifer's to God, is presaged here in his first encounter with authority figures, particularly his aunt Dante who threatens him with eagles (suggesting again images of flight and escape) that will 'pull out his eyes' if he is disobedient, a rhyme derived from a song in Isaac Watts's 1715 *Divine Songs Attempted in Easy Language for the Use of Children*. Aside from the many connections with figures who were violently blinded (such as Oedipus, Tiresias, or Gloucester in *King Lear*), a likely allusion is to Prometheus who was chained to a rock by Zeus, who sent an eagle every day to peck at his liver. Famous as a benefactor to mankind, Prometheus's crime, as was noted earlier in the discussion of *Frankenstein*, was to give human beings fire, against Zeus's command. The allusion again would be made to emphasise Stephen's defiance of authority, and the threat to blind him is in Freudian terms a symbolic threat to castrate him (this opening scene can more generally also be read in terms of Oedipal conflict, from the distinctions Stephen makes between his parents to his attitude towards marrying Eileen).

After the sing-song taunt that has evidently stayed in Stephen's mind, the text is then broken by asterisks to indicate a break in time and scene. It is worth noting that the punctuation used by the narrator in this first section up to the asterisks has been extremely simple, to imitate that of a child, and after the ellipsis at the end of the first sentence has included just full-stops and colons; the only commas have been in the songs and in the speech of adults (l.34 and l.36). Another stylistic feature of Joyce's writing has also been evident: that he uses dashes and not quotation marks to indicate speech. This is because he wanted the speech to appear as a part of the narrative and quotation marks would, he believed, isolate and set off the speech, as though they were quotations introduced into the scenes rather than an integral part of them.

The setting of the story after the asterisks is Stephen's Jesuit school at Clongowes, a stark contrast to the preceding scenes from domestic life. The narrator's choice of language appropriately changes to fit the new environment of rough play ('rude feet': l.51), nicknames ('nasty Roche': l.56), and schoolboy speech ('all the fellows said': ll.54–5). In terms of vocabulary, there is another mention of flight in the football's movement 'like a heavy bird' (1.49), and copious evidence that Stephen will not be the athletic type (his 'weak' eyes suggest reading: 1.53). In these paragraphs the narrator appears to begin by describing the playgrounds in a detached, adult way but moves closer to Stephen as they develop. The habit of referring to Stephen as 'He' and never by name enforces this. By the second paragraph, concerning Rody Kickham and Nasty Roche, the language has become Stephen's again: the sentences are short and simple ('Nasty Roche had big hands' ll.58–9).

Lastly, it is significant that it is only on line 34 that we actually learn the name of the boy who is the subject of the story. The narrator does not tell the reader Stephen's name, but shows it used by others to identify and position him in language: to locate, define and interpellate him. Similarly, at the end of this section we will first learn the boy's surname; again not through the narrator's intervention but on this occasion through Stephen's assertion of it. Nasty Roche's response in the next but one line will be 'What kind of a name is that?' This is an early indication in his life for Stephen that he is different from others; a growing sense of alienation that by the end of the book will culminate in his desire to turn to the ancestor of his surname and to flee Ireland and its constraints: religious, familial, and national.

Further Reading

Beja, Morris (ed.) (1973) *Dubliners and A Portrait of the Artist as a Young Man*, London: Macmillan – now Palgrave.
Ellmann, Richard (19459) *James Joyce*, Oxford: Oxford University Press.
Nolan, Emer (1995) *Joyce and Nationalism*, London: Routledge.
Roughley, A. (1991) *James Joyce and Critical Theory*, Hemel Hempstead: Harvester.

May Sinclair
The Life and Death of
Harriett Frean (1922)

'"Pussycat, Pussycat, where have you been?"
"I've been to London to visit the Queen."
"Pussycat, Pussycat, what did you there?"
"I caught a little mouse under the chair."'

Her mother said it three times. And   5
each time the Baby Harriett laughed.
The sound of her laugh was so funny
that she laughed again at that; she kept
on laughing, with shriller and shriller
squeals.   10
    'I wonder why she thinks it's funny,'
her mother said.
    Her father considered it. 'I don't
know. The cat perhaps. The cat and
the Queen. But no; that isn't funny.'   15
    'She sees something in it we don't
see, bless her,' said her mother.
    Each kissed her in turn, and the Baby
Harriett stopped laughing suddenly.

    'Mamma, did Pussycat see the Queen?'   20
    'No,' said Mamma. 'Just when the
Queen was passing the little mouse came
out of its hole and ran under the chair.
That's what Pussycat saw.'
    Every evening before bedtime she said   25
the rhyme, and Harriett asked the
same question.

    When Nurse had gone she would lie

still in her cot, waiting. The door would
open, the big pointed shadow would   30
move over the ceiling, the lattice shadow
of the fireguard would fade and go away,
and Mamma would come in carrying the
lighted candle. Her face shone white
between the long, hanging curls. She   35
would stoop over the cot and lift Harriett
up, and her face would be hidden in
curls. That was the kiss-me-to-sleep kiss.
And when she had gone Harriett lay
still again, waiting. Presently Papa would   40
come in, large and dark in the firelight.
He stooped and she leapt up into his
arms. That was the kiss-me-awake kiss;
it was their secret.

    Then they played. Papa was the Pussy-   45
cat and she was the little mouse in her
hole under the bedclothes. They played
till Papa said, '*No* more!' And tucked
the blankets tight in.

    'Now you're kissing like Mamma——'   50

    Hours afterwards they would come again
together and stoop over the cot and she
wouldn't see them; they would kiss her
with soft, light kisses, and she wouldn't
know.   55

    She thought: 'To-night I'll stay awake
and see them.' But she never did. Only
once she dreamed that she heard footsteps
and saw the lighted candle, going out of
the room; going, going away.   60

    The blue egg stood on the marble top
of the cabinet where you could see it
from everywhere; it was supported by a
gold waistband, by gold hoops and gold
legs, and it wore a gold ball with a frill   65
round it like a crown. You would never
have guessed what was inside it. You
touched a spring in its waistband and it
flew open, and then it was a workbox.

Gold scissors and thimble and stiletto   70
sitting up in holes cut in white velvet.
    The blue egg was the first thing she
thought of when she came into the room.
There was nothing like that in Connie
Hancock's Papa's house. It belonged to   75
Mamma.
    Harriett thought: 'If only she could
have a birthday and wake up and find
that the blue egg belonged to *her*——'

                                           (London: Virago, 1980)

Sinclair's novella covers the life of her heroine from her birth in 1845 to her death just before the Great War. It is a story of female self-sacrifice, according to Jean Radford in her introduction to the Virago edition, but there is an equally striking way of interpreting the main theme of the text that will have occurred to many readers, and which I will focus on here.

The opening has much in common with the start of Joyce's *A Portrait of the Artist as a Young Man.* Instead of the fairy-tale opening 'Once upon a time', Sinclair uses a nursery rhyme to convey Harriett's first encounter with narrative and language. Just as Stephen Dedalus was the 'baby tuckoo' of his father's story, Harriett plays at being the 'little mouse' of her mother's rhyme (l.46). Harriett laughs at the story her mother tells but her mother does not know why. Her father says he also does not know (ll.13–14), and yet 30 lines later we find that he sometimes plays a game of cat and mouse with Harriett in imitation of the nursery rhyme. It would be easy to conclude that this is why Harriett laughs, imagining herself as the mouse and her father the cat. This is one way to arrive at a reading of what happens in these opening pages. When her father plays the game with Harriett it is their 'secret' (l.44), and the reader alert to this secret between father and daughter will consider there to be more going on in the Frean household than meets the mother's eye.

The first possibility is that Sinclair is interested in illustrating the Electra complex, the female equivalent to the Oedipus complex. There are many suggestions of this, most clearly in the symbolism of her mother's blue egg: 'Harriett thought: "If only she could have a birthday and wake up and find that the blue egg belonged to *her*—"' (ll.77–9). The blue egg, which recurs several times in the novella and which Harriett does indeed come to possess, dominates the room in which it is kept: 'you could see it from everywhere' (ll.62–3). It contains male and female sexual symbols, 'Gold scissors and thimble and stiletto sitting in holes cut in white velvet' (ll.70–1), and is the 'first thing' Harriett thinks of when she comes into the room (ll.72–3). Harriett's desire to possess her mother's egg, combined with the delight she takes in playing cat and mouse with Mr Frean, appears in Freudian terms the normal feeling of an infant girl jealous of her mother's relationship with her father. It also conforms to the Electra complex in that 'She had a belief that her father's house was nicer than other people's houses' (p.9) and that Harriett determines 'She would be like Mamma, and her little girl would be like herself. She couldn't think of it any other way' (p.11).

Sinclair's interest in psychoanalysis is widely known (she was one of the founders of the Medico-Psychological Clinic of London in 1913), and Jean Radford points out that Sinclair 'drew in particular on the Freudian notions of repression and sublimation'. Sinclair was also the first critic to use the term 'stream of consciousness', to describe modernist writers' intensive use of free indirect speech, in relation to the interior monologues in the fiction of her friend Dorothy Richardson. Sinclair's own writing has had this term applied to it but her style is far closer to that of Joyce's *A Portrait* than that of *Ulysses*, published in the same year. The closing pages of *Harriett Frean* can indeed be compared to Molly Bloom's stream-of-consciousness soliloquy at the end of *Ulysses*, the most famous example of stream of consciousness, but Sinclair retains third-person narration throughout the novella and Harriett's darker thoughts are less often glimpsed through preverbal thoughts than through gaps in the narrator's story and especially through Harriett's rambling speech on her death bed: 'She knew that the little man they called the doctor was really Mr Hancock. They oughtn't to have let him in. She cried out, "Take him away. Don't let him touch me ... He oughtn't to do it. Not to *any* woman. If it was known he would be punished"' (p.182).

A further reading of the narrative, which is supported by the above quotation, as with James's *The Turn of the Screw*, suggests that the story is concerned with child abuse. Harriett considers her mother to be angelic: she 'would come in carrying the lighted candle. Her face shone white between her long, hanging curls' (ll.33–5). By contrast her father is pictured as 'large and dark in the firelight' (l.41). Her mother bestows on Harriett a 'kiss-me-to-sleep kiss' (l.38) while her father gives her a 'kiss-me-awake kiss' (l.43), as she leaps 'into his arms' (ll.42–3), and only later starts 'kissing like Mamma' (l.50). The difference between these two types of kiss is left to the reader's imagination. The game Harriett plays with her father has Mr. Frean in the predatory role of the cat while his daughter is 'the little mouse in her hole under the bedclothes' (ll.46–7). Though undoubtedly sexual, at least in the infantile terms of Baby Harriett's desire to usurp her mother's position in her father's affections, such game-playing on the part of the parent may be innocent, or not.

A threat to children is alluded to later in the text when Harriett is warned against going alone into the alley, Black's Lane, at the back of the Freans' house. Here, where inevitably she does stray – even though, or perhaps because, she thinks 'I'm disobeying Mamma' (p.17) – Harriett finds 'something queer, some secret, frightening thing' which proves to be a mysterious man (p.18). We are not told what happens to Harriett when she meets this man: there is a gap in the narrative between her thinking 'She mustn't run' from him, and the time when she arrives back with her mother (p.19). All the reader comes to know for sure about Black's Lane are two things: first, that 'Annie, the housemaid, used to say it was a bad place; something had happened to a little girl there. Annie hushed and reddened and wouldn't tell you what it was' (p.24); second, that years later Harriett, but not the reader, is told the full story by her friend, and while she listens to the revelations Harriett cannot picture the lane other than in terms of her flowers and her mother standing on the garden walk: 'She saw [her mother] all the time while Connie was telling her the secret. She wanted to get up and go to her' (p.25).

Events in Black's Lane may possibly explain why Harriett never marries, though she professes to fall in love with one man, and they may also give rise to the extremely close relationship she develops with Priscilla later in the book. Her attachment to her father may also be the principal reason. Throughout her unmarried life, Harriett idolises her father and only late in the book does she become conscious of the fact that he has not been the paragon of virtue she thought. She learns that he has been responsible for the bankruptcy of not only their own family but also the family of her friend Connie Hancock. Around this time, as though disillusioned with her father and his effect on her life, when Harriett encounters another pussycat later in the story (and this cat is called Mimi as her own was (p.7 and p.157), though the narrative does not make the connection itself) she dislikes the cat intensely and wants it kept away from both herself and her home.

The opening is above all concerned with children's pleasure, and perhaps in particular a delight in repetition: the story is told to her 'three times' (l.5), she asks the same question after hearing the same rhyme each evening (ll.25–7), and her parents follow the same night-time ritual with Harriett, only her father's kiss-me-awake kiss 'was their secret'. It also remains a secret of this heavily symbolic but still enigmatic text what happens in its gaps, ellipses and blank lines. The narrator, who knows more than Harriett does – for example that her parents would 'kiss her with soft, light kisses, and she wouldn't know' (ll.53–5) – keeps the text's secrets to herself, repressing them as they have been repressed in Harriett's mind.

Further Reading

Raitt, Suzanne *May Sinclair: A Modern Victorian*, Oxford: Oxford University Press.

Scott, Bonnie Kime (ed.) (1990) *The Gender of Modernism*, Bloomington: Indiana University Press.

Stevenson, Randall (1992) *Modernist Fiction: An Introduction*, Hemel Hempstead: Harvester.

Zegger, Hrisey Dimitrakis (1976) *May Sinclair*, Boston, MA: Twayne.

E. M. Forster
A Passage to India
(1924)

Except for the Marabar Caves — and they are twenty miles off — the city
of Chandrapore presents nothing extraordinary. Edged rather than
washed by the river Ganges, it trails for a couple of miles along the
bank, scarcely distinguishable from the rubbish it deposits so freely.
There are no bathing-steps on the river front, as the Ganges happens   5
not to be holy here; indeed there is no river front, and bazaars shut out
the wide and shifting panorama of the stream. The streets are mean,
the temples ineffective, and though a few fine houses exist they are
hidden away in gardens or down alleys whose filth deters all but the
invited guest. Chandrapore was never large or beautiful, but two   10
hundred years ago it lay on the road between Upper India, then
imperial, and the sea, and the fine houses date from that period. The
zest for decoration stopped in the eighteenth century, nor was it ever
democratic. In the bazaars there is no painting, and scarcely any
carving. The very wood seems made of mud, the inhabitants of mud   15
moving. So abased, so monotonous is everything that meets the eye,
that when the Ganges comes down it might be expected to wash the
excrescence back into the soil. Houses do fall, people are drowned
and left rotting, but the general outline of the town persists, swelling
here, shrinking there, like some low but indestructible form of life.   20
   Inland, the prospect alters. There is an oval maidan, and a long
sallow hospital. Houses belonging to Eurasians stand on the high
ground by the railway station. Beyond the railway – which runs
parallel to the river – the land sinks, then rises again rather steeply.
On this second rise is laid out the little Civil Station, and viewed hence   25
Chandrapore appears to be a totally different place. It is a city of
gardens. It is no city, but a forest sparsely scattered with huts. It is a
tropical pleasance, washed by a noble river. The toddy palms and
neem trees and mangoes and peepul that were hidden behind the
bazaars now become visible and in their turn hide the bazaars. They   30
rise from the gardens whose ancient tanks nourish them, they burst

out of stifling purlieus and unconsidered temples. Seeking light and
air, and endowed with more strength than man or his works, they
soar above the lower deposit to greet one another with branches and
beckoning leaves, and so build a city for the birds. Especially after the   35
rains do they screen what passes below, but at all times, even when
scorched or leafless, they glorify the city to the English people who
inhabit the rise, so that newcomers cannot believe it to be as meagre as
it is described, and have to be driven down to acquire disillusionment.
As for the Civil Station itself, it provokes no emotion. It charms not,   40
neither does it repel. It is sensibly planned, with a red-brick Club on
its brow, and further back a grocer's and a cemetery, and the bun-
gallows are disposed along roads that intersect at right angles. It has
nothing hideous in it, and only the view is beautiful; it shares nothing
with the city except the overarching sky.   45

The sky too has its changes, but they are less marked than those of
the vegetation and the river. Clouds map it up at times, but it is
normally a dome of blended tints, and the main tint blue. By day the
blue will pale down into white where it touches the white of the land,
after sunset it has a new circumference – orange, melting upwards
into tenderest purple. But the core of blue persists, and so it is by   50
night. Then the stars hang like lamps from the immense vault. The
distance between the earth and them is as nothing to the distance
behind them; and that further distance, though beyond colour, last
freed itself from blue.

The sky settles everything – not only climates and seasons, but   55
when the earth shall be beautiful. By herself she can do little – only
feeble outbursts of flowers. But when the sky chooses, glory can rain
into the Chandrapore bazaars, or a benediction pass from horizon to
horizon. The sky can do this because it is so strong and so enormous.
Strength comes from the sun, infused in it daily, size from the pros-   60
trate earth. No mountains infringe on the curve. League after league
the earth lies flat, heaves a little, is flat again. Only in the south, where
a group of fists and fingers are thrust up through the soil, is the
endless expanse interrupted. These are the fists and fingers of the Marabar
Hills, containing the extraordinary caves.   65

(Harmondsworth: Penguin, 1985)

The opening chapter to *A Passage to India* is only a page and a half in
length and yet most of the major preoccupations of the narrative are
presaged and illustrated in these initial four paragraphs. Forster's
novel begins in mid-sentence, in the sense that the usual order of the

major and minor clauses has been reversed. Instead of writing 'The city of Chandrapore presents nothing extraordinary ... except for the Marabar caves', Forster immediately introduces the central location of the novel and also their chief characteristic: that the caves are exceptional, mysterious, out of the ordinary. It is a common feature of modernist writing (cf. the chapter on *Mrs Dalloway*) to start *in media res*, but Forster's approach throughout this short chapter is transitional, in-between experimental and traditional techniques, because it resembles a realist style (a third-person omniscient narrator introducing the reader systematically to the story's setting) but is heavily symbolic and uses the devices of unusual sentence construction and of description by absence or denial (e.g. 'there is no painting': l.14 and 'It is no city ...': l.27). In this strongly visual introductory two pages the narrator establishes a number of contrasts with which the story is to be concerned. So, the first sentence insists that Chandrapore has *'nothing* extraordinary' but the distant caves, which will curiously not be mentioned again until the very end of the chapter. The opposition here is clearly between the city which presents 'nothing' (as the litany of negatives in the first paragraph amply details) and the 'extraordinary' caves. These two words will occur again and again in the book to express Forster's twin beliefs that existence is astonishing and ultimately meaningless. At the heart of the book's metaphysical concerns is an echoing hollowness which reverberates throughout the narrative – and the caves are the chief symbol of this nullity or vacancy.

The second sentence also begins with a subordinate clause and again establishes a difference: Chandrapore is 'Edged rather than washed'. Forster then accumulates negative images around the city: 'there are no bathing-steps'; 'the Ganges happens not to be holy here'; 'there is no river front'; 'bazaars shut out'; 'streets are mean'; 'temples ineffective'; 'houses ... hidden away'. The 'monotonous' ordinariness of Chandrapore, which was 'never large or beautiful', is pejoratively presented to the point where its filth keeps away all but the 'invited guest'. Here, one of the key social, political, and religious themes of the novel is introduced: that of invitation. The novel is structured around attempts to bring people together: the Bridge party (at which Mrs Bhattacharya encourages Mrs Moore to call on her); Fielding's gathering with Adela, Aziz and Mrs Moore; the invitation to the caves; Godbole's milkmaid's song of invitation to Krishna at Fielding's and his similar invocation on behalf of Mrs Moore at the Gokul Ashtami Festival that starts the third part of the novel. It is integral to Forster's anti-colonial agenda that none of these invitations ends well (even the party at Fielding's is ruined by Ronny): the English are not invited guests in India, and their desire for formality and for forms of exclusion will prevent, as we see at the end of the novel, even Aziz and Fielding from being friends though they both want to be. The political realities of colonialism overpower the force of goodwill which Forster, who famously said he would sooner betray his country than his friend, places at the centre of his liberal humanist philosophy. The paragraph ends by reducing the city to the dirt that results from mixing water and soil, as though the here-unholy Ganges were turning the riverbanks and also the city to sludge: 'The very wood seems made of mud, the inhabitants of mud moving.' The Indian people are figured as 'some low but indestructible form of life', in which phrase Forster reveals his Western conditioning and prejudices but also wishes to convey the fact that Indians inhabited 'their' country for centuries before the arrival of the British, or the Moghuls, and will probably do so for centuries after they have left. Forster's other association here is between land and people – he sees India as a vast country of almost limitless time and space, which dwarfs the islanders of the Raj who hubristically believe they have control and authority over Indian history and territory.

The second paragraph begins to move away from the river – inland – and this is the first example of travelling in the book, which from the first sentence emphasises the distance and the difference between places. The title of the novel, from a poem by Walt Whitman, refers to several journies to India: the English colonial enterprise, Mrs Moore's and Adela's P&O voyage (and Adela's subsequent desire to find the 'real' India), and the train ride to the caves, as well as, metaphorically, the reader's introduction to India by Forster.

It is with the second paragraph that Forster's images of circling and demarcation, inclusion and exclusion come to dominate. On the high ground above Chandrapore are the Eurasians (ll.22–3), who are symbolically positioned between the Indian city and the English Civil Station on the higher second rise. From this vantage point it is possible to see another encampment: 'a city for the birds' in the tall trees (l. 35). All these many communities – Indian, Eurasian, English, and animal – share only 'the overarching sky' (l.45). This 'dome of blending tints' (l.48) is an 'immense vault' (l.51) beyond which there are distances to which 'the distance between the earth and [the stars] is as nothing' (ll.52–3). With these various descriptions, up to the final paragraph, Forster has arranged a series of separations and ever-increasing distances that creates a pattern of arcs moving away from the starting-point of the Ganges.

In a careful progression, the omniscient third-person narration has moved from the (un)holy river through three artificial levels of humanity to the natural animal kingdom and up to the immense vault of the sky, beyond which are still greater distances. The pattern is of circles or arches radiating out from the Ganges as though a pebble had been dropped in the water and the ripples had spread out to encompass each of these places in turn. The major image of the novel that this anticipates is the strange and disturbing echo, 'Ou-boum', that oppresses Mrs Moore and haunts Adela after their experience of the Marabar Caves. One of the explicit links between these tropes is given at the end of chapter V when Mrs Moore decides that 'Outside the arch there seemed always an arch, beyond the remotest echo a silence.' These images are on the one hand of inclusion and encircling and on the other hand they in part suggest the impact of the huge physical geography of India on the English and in part the effect on them of India's spiritual and cultural antiquity.

Forster's novel was received in 1924 as an imaginative and fictional but political treatise on the India question (whether the country should be given Independence), which he denied. Certainly, the book's symbolic and suggestive descriptions seem repeatedly to divide the national characters and religions from each other. The English are physically separate but also emotionally predisposed to segregate and differentiate, a point alluded to by repeated references to 'the roads that intersect at right angles' (1.43). For example, to underline the idea of a gridwork of power and hierarchies, in chapter II we are told that 'The roads, named after victorious generals and intersecting at right angles, were symbolic of the net Great Britain had thrown over India.' Indians and India, however, are associated with invitations and a friendliness which the English take for lack of discrimination, as illustrated by Aziz's insistence on giving his own collar-stud to Fielding at their party in chapter VII, or when we are told that 'no Indian animal has any sense of an interior' at the end of chapter III.

It has been said that 'only connect', the motto of Forster's previous novel *Howards End* (1910), could also be the epigraph to *A Passage to India*. This is partly because the English, though they were proud of an intercontinental *pax Britannica*, were unable after centuries of rule to bring the people of India's two major religions, Hinduism and Islam, into harmony. Emblematic of this, the Collector will attempt and fail to make a bridge between the British colonisers and the Indian colonised with his party in Chapter V. But the novel argues that politics and cultural misunderstandings (Forster calls them 'muddles') will always intrude, and it is only the overarching sky which can connect the 'native' city and the 'sensibly planned' Civil Station – on a physical level, because the sky dictates the heat and dust that India is reduced to in the British imagination and on a metaphysical level because it represents the universal values that Forster believes in, and which are, in the absence of religious unity, summed up in his repeated term 'goodwill' (e.g. see the argument between Mrs Moore and Ronny at the close of Chapter V). The book's tripartite structure reflects this: the parts are called 'Mosque', 'Caves', 'Temple' to represent Islam and Hinduism as bookends between which intervene the ancient pre-deistic caves which seem to have been substituted in this triad for the European Church. The English and their religion have not brought Muslims and Hindus together in India but have instead suffered a crisis of their own religious and moral values (cf. J. G. Farrell's novel *The Siege of Krishnapur*).

In the long second paragraph, after the part-British, part-Indian insertion of the Eurasians, Forster accentuates the difference between the city and the Civil Station. From the second rise Chandrapore appears to be 'no city' but 'a totally different place' (1.26), a forest of huts, gardens and trees; to the extent that it is now 'washed' (1.28) and no longer only edged by the Ganges. Above all this 'soar' the trees which screen the Indians and English from each other because they are 'endowed with more strength than man or his works' (1.33) just as later in the chapter the sky 'is so strong and so enormous' (1.59).

After the detail in the second paragraph about the communities that live above the Indian city, the third paragraph moves to the sky. The dominant subject of the paragraph is colour, and it should strike the reader that up to this point there has been no mention of any colour, except for the 'red-brick Club' (1.41). In this paragraph there are several colours: white, orange, purple and *above all* blue (the colour of not just the sky but also the Hindu god Krishna who Godbole invites to come to him). The sky too has its changes, which are less than those of Chandrapore, but are infinitely greater than those of the distances beyond colour that exist behind the stars. It is with reference to this ultimate scheme of things – the dark, colourless cosmic order – that Forster will describe the petty wranglings of human beings as minuscule and insignificant (which is the conclusion Mrs Moore comes to before the trial, and why, for example, Adela and Fielding are later described as like 'dwarfs shaking hands' in Chapter XXIX). But, at the level of the earth, the important arbiter is the sky, with its many colours, tints, and shades of difference.

It is the sky that forms the weather, so its influence in the novel can be easily noted from the fact that *A Passage to India* proceeds from the initial cold weather of 'Mosque', when everyone is cordial and courteous if cool, to the middle part's hot weather (as metaphor for the passions and tempers aroused by the Marabar Caves incident) and finally the release that comes with the rains of the monsoon in 'Temple'.

So, the last paragraph of chapter I begins by stating that, on earth, the sky settles everything. This idea runs throughout the novel to the very final line's prohibition on a friendship between Aziz and Fielding: 'and the sky said, "No, not there."' On a political level it is arguable therefore that the sky is itself an overarching metaphor for imperial rule – it hangs over the country (the world even) and 'colours' everything that happens beneath, settling whether Indians and Europeans can be friends and when the earth shall be beautiful (1.57), as the 'native' city and the Civil Station (see 1.40) of Chandrapore are not. Underneath this sky, there is only one thing extraordinary to be mentioned in Forster's narrative. There are 'no mountains' (1.61) to break the narrator's camera-eye scanning the landscape, and the earth lies flat *except* where the 'endless expanse [is] interrupted' by the 'fists and fingers' of the Marabar Hills. The narrative has come full circle back to the 'extraordinary caves' that inhabit the hills which stretch up to the sky as though wanting to be reunited (sounding once more the theme of division) with the sun from which Forster speculates in the first paragraph of part two that they were torn ('Caves': Chapter XII).

All the themes and oppositions I have touched on in this discussion of the first chapter recur in later chapters. For example, at the Bridge party there is this paragraph in Chapter IV:

> [The Nawab Bahadur] had spoken in the little room near the courts where the pleaders waited for clients; clients, waiting for pleaders, sat in the dust outside. These had not received a card from Mr Turton. And there were circles even beyond these – people who wore nothing but a loincloth, people who wore not even that, and spent their lives in knocking two sticks together before a scarlet doll – humanity grading and drifting beyond the educated vision, until no earthly invitation can embrace it.

Once more the tropes of invitation, exclusion, circles beyond circles, and humanity's unimportance surface in a chapter which ends with two missionaries debating whether there are sufficient rooms in God's mansion for all people, and for monkeys, and for wasps, or even bacteria (reminding the reader of 'a low but indestructible form of life'): 'No, no this is going too far. We must exclude someone from our gathering, or we shall be left with nothing.' Humans, or at least the English and their religion, must separate, exclude, and compartmentalise, while Forster's narrator says in the first chapter that the sky (the abode of the weather and the gods) can rain 'glory' or pass a benediction 'from horizon to horizon' (ll.57–59). This benign influence of the sky could be seen as also within the power of the Raj over India, but for Forster the political, religious, and social divisions of the Empire amount only to a constricting net of right angles thrown over the subcontinent.

Further Reading

Beer, John (ed.) (1985) *A Passage to India: Essays and Interpretations*, London: Macmillan – now Palgrave.

Bradbury, Malcolm (ed.) (1970) *E. M. Forster: A Passage to India*, London: Macmillan – now Palgrave.

Davies, Tony and Wood, Nigel (eds) (1994) *A Passage to India*, Milton Keynes: Open University.

Dowling, David (1985) *Bloomsbury Aesthetics and the Novels of Forster and Woolf*, London: Macmillan – now Palgrave.

Chapter 16

Virginia Woolf
Mrs Dalloway
(1925)

Mrs Dalloway said she would buy the flowers herself.

For Lucy had her work cut out for her. The doors
would be taken off their hinges; Rumpelmayer's men
were coming. And then, thought Clarissa Dalloway,
what a morning – fresh as if issued to children on a   5
beach.

What a lark! What a plunge! For so it had always
seemed to her when, with a little squeak of the hinges,
which she could hear now, she had burst open the
French windows and plunged at Bourton into the open   10
air. How fresh, how calm, stiller than this of course, the
air was in the early morning; like the flap of a wave;
the kiss of a wave; chill and sharp and yet (for a girl
of eighteen as she then was) solemn, feeling as she did,
standing there at the open window, that something awful   15
was about to happen; looking at the flowers, at the trees
with the smoke winding off them and the rooks rising,
falling; standing and looking until Peter Walsh said,
'Musing among the vegetables?' – was that it? – 'I prefer
men to cauliflowers' – was that it? He must have said it   20
at breakfast one morning when she had gone out on to
the terrace – Peter Walsh. He would be back from India
one of these days, June or July, she forgot which, for
his letters were awfully dull; it was his sayings one
remembered; his eyes, his pocket-knife, his smile, his   25
grumpiness and, when millions of things had utterly
vanished – how strange it was! – a few sayings like this
about cabbages.

She stiffened a little on the kerb, waiting for
Durtnall's van to pass. A charming woman, Scrope Purvis   30
thought her (knowing her as one does know people who live

next door to one in Westminster); a touch of the bird
about her, of the jay, blue-green, light, vivacious, though
she was over fifty, and grown very white since her
illness. There she perched, never seeing him, waiting to   35
cross, very upright.

For having lived in Westminster – how many years
now? over twenty, – one feels even in the midst of the
traffic, or waking at night, Clarissa was positive, a particular hush, or solemnity; an indescribable pause; a sus-   40
pense (but that might be her heart, affected, they said,
by influenza) before Big Ben strikes. There! Out it
boomed. First a warning, musical; then the hour, irrevocable. The leaden circles dissolved in the air. Such
fools we are, she thought, crossing Victoria Street. For   45
Heaven only knows why one loves it so, how one sees it
so, making it up, building it round one, tumbling it,
creating it every moment afresh; but the veriest frumps,
the most dejected of miseries sitting on doorsteps (drink
their downfall) do the same; can't be dealt with, she felt   50
positive, by Acts of Parliament for that very reason:
they love life. In people's eyes, in the swing, tramp, and
trudge; in the bellow and the uproar; the carriages,
motor cars, omnibuses, vans, sandwich men shuffling
and swinging; brass bands; barrel organs; in the triumph   55
and the jingle and the strange high singing of some
aeroplane overhead was what she loved; life; London;
this moment of June.

(Harmondsworth: Penguin, 1992)

Mrs Dalloway, Woolf's first indisputably modernist novel, throws the
reader in at the deep end. The form of the opening sentence, which is
also the first paragraph, is unremarkable and in most respects similar
to the beginning of many realist novels. It is only its immediacy
which is striking, and taken in the context of the following paragraphs, the reader realises that there is not going to be any conventional description of Clarissa Dalloway, no simple account of who
she is, of her family, or of the house where she lives; not even a direct
explanation of why she wants 'the flowers'. Similarly, in the second
paragraph, Lucy is mentioned but not introduced, and while the
reader learns that doors are to be taken off their hinges, presumably
by Rumpelmayer's men, it is not clear why. The reader immediately

has several questions, and it will be many pages before these are answered, but in the meantime the reader will move in and out of the mind of Clarissa Dalloway, as well as others, gathering information through the thoughts and impressions of one hot day in June 1923. In other words, Woolf chooses to 'plunge' (l.7) the reader into the novel just as Mrs Dalloway 'plunged' into the open air at Bourton (l.10). As in 'life' (l.57), which is the primary subject of Woolf's novel, readers have to orientate themselves while trying to understand events and people they are encountering for the first time.

The third paragraph moves the narrative into the past at Bourton and it is important to realise how Woolf takes Clarissa there; or rather how Clarissa takes herself back there. The association is made by the hinges of the doors to be removed (l.3) and the squeaky hinges at Bourton (l.8). This is a fact which, retrospectively, confirms for the reader that, though the book's opening sentence was a direct statement by the narrator (unless it was a thought of Lucy's), from the second paragraph on the narrator has been mediating the thoughts of Mrs Dalloway. This introduces the features of Woolf's particular narrative style, which is to use a third-person narrator but also a considerable amount of indirect speech and accompanying tags ('thought Clarissa Dalloway': l.4). Woolf also employs, as in this third paragraph, extensive interior monologue, but the thoughts are usually still presented in the third person, mediated by the narrator, such as 'one of these days, June or July, she forgot which' (l.23). It is a peculiar strength of Woolf's narrative technique that she is able to move between characters' minds almost imperceptibly (consider the transitions between paragraphs 3, 4 and 5). This is largely because of her third-person narration, her use of 'one' instead of 'I', and her choice of similar vocabulary and images for every person (James Joyce is very different in this respect), but it would be impossible without her use of indirect reporting, in which no quotation marks are used to represent speech or thought. The prose appears seamless as it floats between the characters and the narrator, with only the tags to confirm for the reader whose thoughts or opinions are being offered.

The third paragraph provides the first examples of many phrases and images which will become familiar during the course of the book. For example 'plunge' (l.7) is a word with two particular associations: first, with the action of the mind as it 'plunges' into memory, as Clarissa does here (Woolf throughout the novel gives images of a bird diving down through air or water to suggest the mind's plunge below the surface); second, with the major event of the novel – the shell-shocked soldier Septimus Smith's fatal 'plunge' from a window (p.202), news of which intrudes on Clarissa's party that evening (the reason for the flowers of line 1) and causes her to reflect upon death's various significances in life. It is this event which Clarissa anticipates in her sensation that 'something awful was about to happen' (in an earlier plan of the book, Clarissa was to commit suicide herself, but Woolf introduced Septimus as her male double). Clarissa's premonition of death, which is with her throughout the day, also reminds the reader of the recent war, which hangs over the story like a cloud darkening the lives of all the characters, even though many of them want to feel it is firmly behind them by 1923. Lastly in this paragraph, the third most important character in the novel, after Clarissa and Septimus, is introduced: Peter Walsh. Also, the personal possession we will come to associate with him is mentioned in line 25: his pocket-knife. The knife, with which Peter is always fiddling, is obviously a phallic symbol (like Big Ben later in the passage), but it is also another emblem of the past as it comes to remind the reader of a weapon usually associated with the Great War and particularly with crossing no-man's-land: the bayonet. The blade can be opened or closed, as a bayonet can be attached to, or detached from, a rifle. Most pertinently, the pocket-knife is also reminiscent of the bayonet-like railings on which, to escape the horror of the war which continues to haunt him, Septimus impales himself at the book's close. Another distinctly modernist feature is in evidence in the paragraph in connection with Peter. The phrase associated with him, 'I prefer men to cauliflowers, – was that it?' (l.19–20), is casually mentioned here only to resurface, corrected, over 200 pages later at the end of the novel: 'he did not like cabbages; he preferred human beings, Peter said' (p.211). It is typical of modernist novels that the reader has to make such distant connections across the narrative, as though the book were not laid out in sequential pages but held in the mind as a whole, available all at once. The tricks played by memory are also suggested on this opening page by the change in Clarissa's mind from 'cauliflowers' (l.20) to 'cabbages' (l.28) in the third paragraph.

In the fourth paragraph, the narrator moves away from Clarissa's thoughts and focalises the narrative through the mind of one of her neighbours, the improbably named Scrope Purvis, who views her from across the street. He thinks of Clarissa as 'perched' (l.35) on the kerb like a bird, and this is one of the key images which will come to be associated with her. She is thought here to be upright, light, and vivacious like a jay (and, incidentally, earlier in the story there has already been mention of rooks (1.17) and, obliquely, a lark: (1.7)). Bird imagery is used by Woolf, as I have mentioned, generally to illustrate the fluid, floating movement of the mind, but specifically to suggest Clarissa's fragility, timidity and unusual grace.

The last paragraph returns to Clarissa's thoughts and brings to the fore several of the central preoccupations of the novel. The snaking first sentence enacts its own subject. It is a prolonged and delayed progression towards the moment when 'Big Ben strikes' – the long sentence is itself an exercise in 'suspense' (ll.40–1). The masculine (all objects were gendered for Woolf) Westminster clock then 'booms' out, 'first a warning' then the hour 'irrevocable' (ll. 42–4). The suggestion of a gun or cannon having fired is underlined by the following sentence: 'The leaden circles dissolved in the air.' This common phrase in the novel may remind the attentive reader of the war and it may also suggest the way in which Woolf attempts to encircle all her characters. The striking of a clock is her standard device in *Mrs Dalloway* to move her narrator from one character's thoughts to another's, as they both hear the sound wherever they are in central London – the chiming intrudes on their personal thoughts and brings them alive to the public life, and time, in which they all participate. It is this encompassing, shared experience of life that Clarissa, mediated by the narrator, begins to imagine in the rest of the paragraph. For Woolf, life surrounds and assails the individual's senses, such that each of us is 'building it', 'tumbling it', 'creating it every moment afresh' (ll.47–8). Life is dynamic, exciting, overpowering: a constant bombardment of sensations. Famously, Woolf wrote in one of her essays that:

> The mind receives a myriad impressions – trivial, fantastic, evanescent, or engraved with the sharpness of steel. From all sides they come, an incessant shower of innumerable atoms ... Life is not a series of gig-lamps symmetrically arranged; life is a luminous halo, a semi-transparent envelope that surrounds us from the beginning of consciousness to the end. ('Modern Fiction', 1919)

This is the impression that is conveyed in the final sentence of this opening, in prose that attempts to stretch the linear form of writing to its limit and give the reader the impression that the sights and sounds of London are impinging on Clarissa at one moment:

> In people's eyes, in the swing, tramp, and trudge; in the bellow and the uproar; the carriages, motor cars, omnibuses, vans, sandwich men shuf-

fling and swinging; brass bands; barrel organs; in the triumph and the jingle and the strange high singing of some aeroplane overhead was what she loved; life; London; this moment of June.

The passage has built to a climax to suggest the experience of all of these sights and sounds overwhelming Clarissa at once.

To stress the importance of this intense feeling, I want now to consider a more vehement example from later in the book. It is in a passage which tries to make real for the reader a word which has, somewhat unusually, appeared twice in the last paragraph of the opening: the 'moment' (a special term for Woolf, who uses it 70 times in the novel). The passage occurs when Clarissa exchanges a kiss with Sally Seton at Bourton:

> It was a sudden revelation, a tinge like a blush which one tried to check and then, as it spread, one yielded to its expansion, and rushed to the farthest verge and there quivered and felt the world come closer, swollen with some astonishing significance, some pressure of rapture, which split its thin skin and gushed and poured with an extraordinary alleviation over the cracks and sores. Then, for that moment, she had seen an illumination; a match burning in a crocus; an inner meaning almost expressed. But the close withdrew; the hard softened. It was over – the moment. (pp. 34–5)

For Woolf the 'moment' is an expression of 'life', in which it is a connecting force, a common, heightened almost healing sensation (which is something Woolf's depiction of shared, similar thought also aims to include). Clarissa's kiss with Sally is the most deeply felt expression of the 'moment' in *Mrs Dalloway*, and it very clearly has an almost orgasmic intensity. The passage, like much of the novel, describes the physicality of emotional experience, just as the last paragraph of the opening has tried to build up the emotional force for Clarissa of being alive at one 'moment of June'.

I mentioned at the start of this chapter that modernist novels do not provide direct descriptions and simple details of characters' lives; and yet an attentive reader has actually learned a great deal about Mrs Dalloway in the opening paragraphs: that she lives in Westminster (1.37), and has done for over 20 years (1.38), that she is over 50 (1.34), has been ill (11.34–5), probably with influenza (1.42), has white hair (1.34) and is bird-like in appearance. From the last paragraph, and its talk of 'the veriest frumps' and drunken 'miseries', the reader has also gained an initial idea of her social views. The rest of the novel continues to accrete information about Clarissa, up to the final statement of the narrative: 'For there she was.' This ultimate comment refers less to her presence at her party than to the fact that over 200 pages she has been carefully and fully revealed to the reader in all her ordinariness and her uniqueness. Like many modernist texts, if readers remember its title or its opening two words they should find that *Mrs Dalloway* has come full circle: for there she was (see spatial reading in the glossary).

Further Reading

Bowlby, Rachel (1988) *Virginia Woolf: Feminist Destinations*, Oxford: Basil Blackwell.

Dowling, David (1991) *Mrs Dalloway: Mapping Stream of Consciousness*, Boston, MA: Twayne.

Kolocotroni, Vassiliki, Goldman, Jane and Taxidou, Olga (eds) (1998) *Modernism: An Anthology of Sources and Documents*, Edinburgh: Edinburgh University Press (including an extract from Woolf's 'Modern Fiction', p.397).

Reid, Su (ed.) (1993) *Mrs Dalloway and To the Lighthouse*, London: Macmillan – now Palgrave.

Aldous Huxley
Brave New World
(1932)

A squat grey building of only thirty-four storeys. Over the main
entrance the words, CENTRAL LONDON HATCHERY AND CON-
DITIONING CENTRE, and, in a shield, the World State's motto,
COMMUNITY, IDENTITY, STABILITY.

The enormous room on the ground floor faced towards the north.   5
Cold for all the summer beyond the panes, for all the tropical heat of
the room itself, a harsh thin light glared through the windows,
hungrily seeking some draped lay figure, some pallid shape of academic goose-flesh, but finding only the glass and nickel and bleakly
shining porcelain of a laboratory. Wintriness responded to wintri-   10
ness. The overalls of the workers were white, their hands gloved
with a pale corpse-coloured rubber. The light was frozen, dead, a
ghost. Only from the yellow barrels of the microscopes did it bor-
row a certain rich and living substance, lying along the polished
tubes like butter, streak after luscious streak in long recession down   15
the work tables.

'And this', said the Director opening the door, 'is the Fertilizing
Room.'

Bent over their instruments, three hundred Fertilizers were
plunged, as the Director of Hatcheries and Conditioning entered   20
the room, in the scarcely breathing silence, the absent-minded soli-
loquizing hum or whistle, of absorbed concentration. A troop of
newly arrived students, very young, pink and callow, followed ner-
vously, rather abjectly, at the Director's heels. Each of them carried
a note-book, in which, whenever the great man spoke, he desper-   25
ately scribbled. Straight from the horse's mouth. It was a rare privilege. The D.H.C. For Central London always made a point of personally conducting his new students round the various departments.

'Just to give you a general idea,' he would explain to them. For
of course some sort of general idea they must have, if they were to   30
do their work intelligently – though as little of one, if they were to

be good and happy members of society, as possible. For particulars, as everyone knows, make for virtue and happiness; generalities are intellectually necessary evils. Not philosophers, but fret-sawyers and stamp collectors compose the backbone of society.   35

'Tomorrow', he would add, smiling at them with a slightly menacing geniality, 'you will be settling down to serious work. You won't have time for generalities. Meanwhile ...'

Meanwhile, it was a privilege. Straight from the horse's mouth into the note-book. The boys scribbled like mad.   40

Tall and rather thin but upright, the Director advanced into the room. He had a rather long chin and big, rather prominent teeth, just covered, when he was not talking, by his full, floridly curved lips. Old, young? Thirty? fifty? fifty-five? It was hard to say. And any-how the question didn't arise; in this year of stability, A.F. 632, it   45
didn't occur to you to ask it.

'I shall begin at the beginning,' said the D.H.C., and the more zealous students recorded his intention in their note-books: *Begin at the Beginning*. 'These,' he waved his hand, 'are the incubators.' And opening an insulated door he showed them racks upon racks   50
of numbered test-tubes. 'This week's supply of ova. Kept', he ex-plained, 'at blood heat; whereas the male gametes,' and here he opened another door, 'they have to be kept at thirty-five instead of thirty-seven. Full blood heat sterilizes.' Rams wrapped in thermo-gene beget no lambs.   55

(Harmondsworth: Penguin, 1955)

Brave New World takes its title from Miranda's comment on her first encounter with wider humanity in Shakespeare's *The Tempest*: 'How beauteous mankind is! O brave new world,/That has such people in't' (Act V, scene i, line 183). Huxley's novel takes up this theme of the 'vision' of a new society and constructs a fable centred on a world state 600 years in the future where social stability is based on a scientific caste system. Human beings, graded from highest intellec-tuals to lowest manual workers, hatched from incubators and brought up in communal nurseries, learn by methodical condi-tioning to accept their social destiny. The novel's main character is Bernard Marx, an unorthodox and therefore unhappy alpha-plus, who visits a New Mexican reservation and brings a 'savage' back to London. The 'savage' is at first fascinated by the 'new world', like Miranda, but finally revolted, and his argument with Mustapha Mond, world controller, demonstrates the incompatibility of individual freedom and a scientifically trouble-free society (like most names in the novel, the world controller's is taken from a figure who changed society: Alfred Mond (1868–1930) was a British industrialist and politician who became the first commissioner of works, minister of health, and a founder of ICI). Huxley writes that the book is about the advancement of science as it affects human individuals. Seriously as well as satirically, it amalgamates eugenics, psychoanalysis, mass entertainment, and the factory production-line in an attempt to present a dystopia which is less of a prediction of life in the future than a warning about the excesses of the present (like Wells's *The Time Machine* and Orwell's *1984*). One of its main concerns is the 'standardisation' of people as theories of 'humanity' overwhelm actual cultural and social difference. Huxley's fear seems to be that happiness and material well-being will be bought at the price of diversity and individuality.

His targets in the novel are various: the reduction of human emotional complexity and social diversity to simple drives and neuroses; the cult of perpetual youth, and its attendant denigration of the old; the deleterious effects of increased leisure; the influence of production-line work-tasks, which leads to purely vocational training and extreme specialism; the development of eugenics and selective breeding; Pavlovian behaviourism; the dangerous mix of a dogmatic egalitarianism and a rabid consumerism.

A more specific theory among critics about the target of *Brave New World* argues that Huxley had in mind contemporary Los Angeles when he wrote the novel. He had visited California in the 1920s and thought it a place in which everyone was happy but there was no intellectual life or purpose. In an essay called 'The Outlook for American Culture, Some Reflections in a Machine Age', he wrote that the American way of life encompassed a large majority of people who 'do not want to be cultured, are not interested in the higher life. For these people existence on the lower, animal levels is perfectly satisfactory. Given food, drink, the company of their fellows, sexual enjoyment, and plenty of noisy distractions from without, they are happy.' He continued: 'all the resources of science are applied in order that imbecility may flourish and vulgarity cover the whole earth'. Huxley found the ordinary to be exalted above the extraordinary, and there was an increasing intellectual standardisation. Consequently, in *Brave New World* there is no existence outside the collective state, and the goal of this community is little more than the satisfaction of animal desires, amounting to a state of institutionalised dependency which Huxley saw as in many ways the antithesis of freedom. The society in the book is a parody of the model for the state in Plato's *Republic* in that there is a governing elite ('guardians' as Plato calls them) overseeing five castes: but importantly the castes are not just divided socially but biologically. As the Controller observes, people have nothing to get excited about: no significant others, no illnesses, no crime or violence, and no family. 'Mother' and 'Father' are now swear words. There is also no religion, no art, no philosophy and no poetry. Literature is thought to promote unhappiness: as though anticipating an extreme political correctness the authorities in *Brave New World* argue that Hamlet and Othello glorify private murder. Literature is also a form of escapism and in this perfectly ordered and adjusted society there is nothing for the chemically designed people to escape from.

It is clear from the opening paragraphs that the reduction of life to its most basic drives and desires is ultimately the society of *Brave New World*'s most stultifying and oppressive aspect. The sense of a towering Metropolis is created by the first sentence which describes a 'squat' building that is '*only* thirty-four storeys', suggesting most buildings are much higher, while the drab homogeneity of this future life is hinted at in the fact that the building is 'grey'. It is perhaps also indicative of the debasement of language that both this and the next sentence do not have a complete sense in that they lack verbs, and so are not strictly speaking sentences at all. The corporate pride and self-aggrandisement of this *Brave New World* are implied by the name and shield over the main entrance to the Hatchery and Conditioning Centre. That it is in 'central London' places the building at the heart of the Imperial capital, as London still was in 1932, underlining the building's importance. Also, the fact that the World State has a motto, unlike any present-day country, implies that it is itself more like an institution, club or company. The words of the motto are conservative and traditionalist, opposed to change in terms of the collective (Community), the individual (Identity), and the status quo (Stability).

The second paragraph concerns the clinical atmosphere within the Hatchery; its chief concern is with light, probably because light, with its heat (see lines 52–5), is the primary source of life on earth, without which no plant would grow or egg 'hatch'. The room faces not the warm south but north (1.5) and admits 'harsh thin light' (1.7), that is 'cold for all the summer beyond the panes' (1.6), to 'pallid' shapes (1.8) and 'bleakly shining porcelain' (ll.9–10). The phrase 'Wintriness responded to wintriness' implies that the cold, sterile artificiality of the Hatchery taints the natural light that the narrator says 'glared' (l.7) through the window. In the next two sentences the people and the light are matched: the overalls are 'white', the light 'frozen'; the gloves 'pale', the light 'a ghost'; the rubber 'corpse-coloured', the light 'dead' (ll.11–13). The mention of a 'corpse' contrasts and links with the image of the human eggs: the 'rich and living substance, lying along the polished tubes like butter, streak after streak in long recession down the work tables' (ll.14–16) in the following sentence. Both are about 'the light' but suggest the idea of people laid out like slabs of meat (or the 'draped lay figure' of line 8), connoting not birth but death (as does the 'scarcely breathing silence' of the next paragraph, in l. 21). All this leads into the first, ironic, spoken words of the book, that this 'is the Fertilizing Room' (l.17–18). By this point it is clear that the purpose of the description of the Fertilizing Room is to contrast with the idea of 'natural' human procreation, which is associated with warmth, intimacy and love.

Inside the room, Huxley creates a picture of a human factory-production system as 'three hundred Fertilizers' are 'bent' and 'plunged' in 'absorbed concentration' over their microscopes (ll.19–22). The 'very young, pink and callow' (l.23) students who come in after the Director form a 'troop' (l.22) whose extreme youth and freshness echoes the theme of new life, and introduces the 'academic goose-flesh' sought by the light earlier (ll.8–9). The students (all male) themselves seem reverential, sycophantic and abject in their nervousness before 'the great man' (l.25), presaging the book's adoration of Henry Ford ('A.F.' in line 45 refers to 'After Ford', which has replaced Anno Domini or Common Era, just as in the novel prayers are to Our Ford, not Our Lord, and the Model T has replaced the Christian cross).

The fourth paragraph begins to map out the beliefs of the World State. It is for particularities and against generalities, pro intelligence but not intellectualism, in favour of 'good and happy' productive workers but wary of the 'necessary evils' brought by thinkers. That 'fret-sawyers and stamp-collectors compose the backbone of society' is a significant metaphor as the Director is speaking in the room where genetic designs are composed and anatomical characteristics are engineered. The fifth paragraph underlines this by suggesting that study is not 'serious work' and that the students should consider themselves both privileged and unformed; they are embryonic or ignorant, and in need of not abstract, potentially harmful theories (generalities) but the director's concrete, scientific experience.

The following paragraph is primarily a description of the Director, who is himself comparable to a test-tube: 'Tall and rather thin but upright'. His features seem reminiscent of a wolf or similar animal, with a long chin/snout, large prominent teeth, and full, petal-like lips. It is also significant that Huxley only describes the lower half of the Director's face, around his mouth: first because the students are concentrating on him as an orator and second because no further suggestion of personality can be given by a description of his hair, nose, or especially eyes. His age is immaterial because of the society's and the people's lack of change, which is promoted as 'stability' (l.45) and identity in the World State motto.

In the final paragraph, the Director stresses beginnings, surrounded by the test-tube examples of conception, but ironically he also describes a system which cuts off children from parents, people from roots, individuals from ancestry. The expression 'Full blood heat sterilizes' (l.54) ominously suggests the danger of uncontrolled reproduction, and the importance of taking the process away from the passion of individual couples.

Huxley, when he was working on the novel, described it in a letter as:

> a comic or at least satirical, novel about the future, showing the appalling-ness (at any rate by our standards) of Utopia and adumbrating the effects on thought and feeling of such quite possible biological inventions as the production of children in bottles (with consequent abolition of the family and all the Freudian 'complexes' for which family relationships are responsible), the prolongation of youth, the devising of some harmless but effective substitute for alcohol, cocaine, opium etc: – and also the effects of such sociological reforms on Pavlovian conditions of all children from birth and before birth, universal peace, security and stability.

Such a vision is evidently clear in the novel's opening where the womb is substituted by tubes in a carefully controlled production-line laboratory, replacing nature and family with scientific, patriarchal instrumentalism and programmed fertilisation. Of all the dystopian visions produced before the Second World War *Brave New World* is probably the one which has most relevance to the media-saturated consumer society of multi-national globalisation after it (a 'dystopia', a term coined by the nineteenth-century philosopher John Stuart Mill, is a fictitious place where everything is as bad as the author can envisage, in opposition to a Utopia, where everything is as good as the author can imagine).

Further Reading

Baker, Robert S. (1990) *Brave New World: History, Science and Dystopia*, Boston, MA: Twayne.

Deery, June (1996) *Aldous Huxley and the Mysticism of Science*, London: Macmillan – now Palgrave.

Greenblatt, Stephen Jay (1965) *Three Modern Satirists: Waugh, Orwell, and Huxley*, Hew Haven, CT and London: Yale University Press.

Woodcock, George (1972) *Dawn and the Darkest Hour*, London: Faber & Faber.

Chapter 18

George Orwell
The Road to Wigan Pier
(1937)

The first sound in the mornings was the clumping of the
mill-girls' clogs down the cobbled street. Earlier than that,
I suppose, there were factory whistles which I was never
awake to hear.

There were generally four of us in the bedroom, and a   5
beastly place it was, with that defiled impermanent look of
rooms that are not serving their rightful purpose. Years
earlier the house had been an ordinary dwelling-house, and
when the Brookers had taken it and fitted it out as a tripe-
shop and lodging house, they had inherited some of the   10
more useless pieces of furniture and had never had the
energy to remove them. We were therefore sleeping in what
was still recognizably a drawing-room. Hanging from the
ceiling there was a heavy glass chandelier on which the
dust was so thick that it was like fur. And covering most of   15
one wall there was a huge hideous piece of junk, something
between a sideboard and a hall-stand, with lots of carving
and little drawers and strips of looking-glass, and there was a
once-gaudy carpet ringed by the slop-pails of years, and two
gilt chairs with burst seats, and one of those old-fashioned   20
horsehair armchairs which you slide off when you try to sit
on them. The room had been turned into a bedroom by
thrusting four squalid beds in among this other wreckage.

My bed was in the right-hand corner on the side nearest
the door. There was another bed across the foot of it and   25
jammed hard against it (it had to be in that position to
allow the door to open) so that I had to sleep with my legs
doubled up; if I straightened them out I kicked the occupant of the other bed in the small of the back. He was
an elderly man named Mr Reilly, a mechanic of sorts and   30
employed 'on top' at one of the coal pits. Luckily he had

to go to work at five in the morning, so I could uncoil my
legs and have a couple of hours' proper sleep after he was
gone. In the bed opposite there was a Scotch miner who
had been injured in a pit accident (a huge chunk of stone   35
pinned him to the ground and it was a couple of hours
before they could lever it off), and had received five hundred
pounds compensation. He was a big handsome man of forty,
with grizzled hair and a clipped moustache, more like a
sergeant-major than a miner, and he would lie in bed till   40
late in the day, smoking a short pipe. The other bed was
occupied by a succession of commercial travellers, news-
paper-canvassers, and hire-purchase touts who generally
stayed for a couple of nights. It was a double bed and much
the best in the room. I had slept in it myself my first night   45
there, but had been manoeuvred out of it to make room for
another lodger. I believe all newcomers spent their first
night in the double bed, which was used, so to speak, as
bait. All the windows were kept tight shut, with a red sandbag jammed in the bottom, and in the morning the room   50
stank like a ferret's cage. You did not notice it when you
got up, but if you went out of the room and came back, the
smell hit you in the face with a smack.

(Harmondsworth: Penguin, 1962)

Orwell was commissioned to write *The Road to Wigan Pier* for the Left Book Club (founded in 1936 by Victor Gollancz, who had published Orwell's earlier novels), which had a membership of around 50 000 in 1937. Gollancz wanted a report on the conditions of unemployed miners in Lancashire and Yorkshire, and chose Orwell as a committed and sympathetic author (Orwell had written in his 1935 novel *A Clergyman's Daughter* that there was an eleventh modern commandment: 'Thou shalt not lose thy job'). The first half of *The Road to Wigan Pier* is Orwell's account, just as Gollancz wanted. However, Gollancz also received, in the second half of the book, Orwell's personal assessment of socialism, poverty, his own upbringing and England's economic and cultural malaise.

The first part of *The Road to Wigan Pier* is based on Orwell's eight-week tour of the north of England at the end of 1936; by the time it was published he was in Spain, offering to fight for the government in the Civil War. In the meantime the Left Book Club had asked for many changes to the manuscript, but Orwell refused to alter a word and Gollancz decided to publish the book with a foreword: one which praised the first half of the book but distanced the Club from the idiosyncratic views expressed in the second half. Despite its publisher's reservations, it soon became the Club's best seller and generated more discussion than any of its other books.

The Road to Wigan Pier is not a novel; it is classified by Penguin as 'autobiography'. However, it is a written by a novelist, who has admitted that he invented details, and it employs many of the devices of fiction. History, journalism and essays (a form of prose Orwell excelled at) all use narrative, imagery, metaphors, selection and other superficially 'literary' techniques. For example, Orwell's first sentence uses alliteration in its repetition of hard 'c' and 'l' and 'g' sounds: 'the clumping of the mill-girls' clogs down the cobbled street'. Additionally, Orwell is using language to imitate the sound he is describing, creating a rhythmical onomatopoeic sentence. It then emerges that this initial sound is only the first that he hears, and that earlier whistles have probably signalled the start of the work day for others. In this opening paragraph Orwell has placed the importance of work at the centre of his book by devoting one sentence to the mills and another to the factories.

The second paragraph catalogues the 'wreckage' (1.23) Orwell laments in his 'defiled' (1.6) bedroom: 'useless' (1.11) furniture, 'hideous' (1.16) junk, 'once-gaudy' (1.19) carpet, 'burst' (1.20) seats, and an 'old-fashioned' (1.20) horsehair armchair he slides off. The whole is summed up in a characteristic Orwellian word: 'beastly' (1.6). It is as though Orwell has consulted a thesaurus to find every word of debasement or obsolescence he can use in turn. The way the room is described, the passage's repeated motifs and its imagery, imply a particular viewpoint throughout. In words like 'beastly'(1.6) and 'fur' (1.15), along with others such as 'defiled' (1.6) and 'squalid' (1.23), Orwell also conveys his feeling of degraded and reduced humanity in what he later calls a 'ferret's cage' (1.51), though this has been seen by several critics to show his personal dislike of the Brookers' house. It is significant that the major object in the room Orwell describes is unnamable, being a cross 'between a sideboard and a hall-stand' (1.17); and this fits with the various descriptions of all the pieces of furniture: none fulfils a purpose, creating a general impression of uselessness and redundancy (even the room is a drawing-room which has been turned into a bedroom simply by sticking in it 'four squalid beds': 1. 23). That the hybrid piece of junk is 'huge' and occupies 'most of one wall' (1.15–6) makes its pointlessness appear all the more frustrating in the excessively cramped conditions. The one simile in the second paragraph, dust 'like fur' (l.15), connects with the mild suggestion of inhumanity.

This is Orwell's chief point: he wants the Left Book Club readers to be indignant at the inhumane conditions in which he is forced to live, with his three fellow lodgers in the same room. Orwell once commented: 'when you go to the industrial north, you are conscious ... of entering another country' and this is how the north would be viewed by his southern, highly educated, left-wing readers (for example, Liverpool had twice as many people as London living below subsistence level in 1930). However, as the first chapter develops it becomes less clear whether Orwell is appalled by the social fact of such a life, or by the squalor embraced by the Brooker family who own and run the house. Who is to blame for the 'squalid' beds (l.23) and for the fact that the room is not being used for its 'rightful purpose' (l.7)? While the Brookers are tripe-shop owners, they are also landlords.

It is the third paragraph that moves on to describe life in the room rather than the objects. Orwell shares the 'bedroom' with three other men: one is 'elderly' (l.30) and another is 'injured' (l.35), while the identity of the third occupant is constantly changing between travellers, canvassers and touts: this creates the impression more of a hospital than a boarding-house, and there is a strange blend of the impressions of permanency and itinerancy, which is exacerbated by the fact that the occupants of the room have to change beds when a newcomer arrives and is tempted to stay on by the Brookers with the double. After Orwell's early statement that he has to sleep with his legs 'doubled up' (l.28), the feeling of confinement, almost of a barracks (note the sergeant-major comparison in line 40), is heightened by the claustrophobic effect of the windows being 'kept tight shut' (l.49) and the *sandbag* 'jammed' in at the bottom.

As has been noted of Orwell's writings generally, it is smells that bother his class sensibilities most about living at the Brookers' lodging-house (cf. '*The lower classes smell*' on p.112). He finishes this paragraph by comparing the room's 'stink' to that of a 'ferret's cage' (l.51) again suggesting animality through a simile (as does the double bed used 'as bait': ll.48–9). That it is 'beastly' and brutal is emphasised by the closing line's statement that the smell hits '*you* in the face with a smack' (l.53). The violence returns the reader to the details which started the paragraph: 'I had to sleep with my legs doubled up; if I straightened them out I kicked the occupant of the other bed in the small of the back' (l.27–9).

The Road to Wigan Pier, though not fiction, is in many respects representative of the style of writing which in literary discussions in the 1930s challenged the innovatory techniques of writers such as James Joyce and Virginia Woolf. In general, unlike modernist writing, 1930s texts are not associated with innovation, defamiliarisation, formalism, philosophy or the foregrounding of individual consciousness. Experimental writing was out of fashion. There is instead in 1930s writing a return to popularity of omnisicent third-person narration (in Orwell's case here it is first-person but authoritative, and favours a documentary style). Such texts concentrate on the here and now, with ordinary people in recognisable towns and villages. In general terms it was thought by 1930s writers that literature should be about everybody, for everybody, which meant using modes of writing based on realist models. In terms of form and style, literary texts were often modelled on historical or journalistic techniques: autobiography, the eye-witness account, the journal, the diary (representative titles include *Journey to a War, Berlin Diary, Journey without Maps*). Orwell's book stands at the centre of this trend as it is a novelist's attempt to write a documentary account of what it is like 'going over' from the privileged, cultured elite to the working class. Novelists talked of offering a window on to a common shared, objective reality, not an intense vision of a subjective, aestheticised world. There is also a tendency in their writing to reduce groups to representative individuals, politicial parties to policies, wars to weapons (for example, texts are more likely to include a reference to workers as hands, a metonym, than drones, a metaphor).

The 1930s contained a literary change to parallel a political shift. Orwell writes in 'Inside the Whale', his essay about literature in the 1930s:

> quite suddenly, in the years 1930–35, something happens, the literary climate changes. A new group of writers, Auden and Spender and the rest of them, has made its appearance, and although technically these writers owe something to their predecessors, their 'tendency' is entirely different. Suddenly we have got out of the twilight of the gods into a sort of boy scout atmosphere of bare knees and community singing. The typical literary man ceases to be a cultured expatriate with a leaning towards the church and becomes instead an eager-minded schoolboy with a leaning towards communism. If the keynote of the writers of the twenties is 'tragic sense of life', the keynote of the new writers is 'serious purpose'.

Orwell's other valid criticism in the essay is that most writers toy with communist politics without having the vaguest idea of what it is like to be poor or to be subject to a communist government.

Typically, at the margins of Left-wing thinkers, he observes that it is easy to play at being 'political' in a liberal society, as many intellectuals did in the 1930s, but much harder for upper- and middle-class writers to live among the workers. Orwell is thus unusual in that he did go *Down and Out in Paris and London* (1933), took *The Road to Wigan Pier* and fought in Spain (see his *Homage to Catalonia*, 1938).

Lastly, the title of Orwell's book works on three levels. It evidently refers to Orwell's literal journey north; it suggests the road that has to be metaphorically travelled by the middle-class readers of the Left Book Club if they wish to follow their socialist principles; and it alludes to the music-hall stereotyping of Wigan, a northern working-class mining town which built itself a pier on the Leeds to Liverpool canal to attract holidaymakers who might not want to trek all the way to Blackpool. Orwell composed the book in the tradition of Engels' *Condition of the Working-Class in England in 1844* and Jack London's *People of the Abyss* (1903). His reward for writing the most famous of many accounts of working-class life in the 1930s is now to have the pub on Wigan Pier named after him.

Further Reading

Cunningham, Valentine (1990) *British Writers of the Thirties*, Oxford: Oxford University Press.

Fowler, Roger (1995) *The Language of George Orwell*, London: Macmillan – now Palgrave.

Hynes, Samuel (1972) *The Auden Generation*, London: Faber & Faber.

Orwell, George (1970) *The Collected Essays, Journalism and Letters of George Orwell* (eds. Sonia Orwell and Ian Angus), 4 vols, Harmondsworth: Penguin.

Christopher Isherwood
Goodbye to Berlin
(1939)

From my window, the deep solemn massive street.
Cellar-shops where the lamps burn all day, under the
shadow of top-heavy balconied façades, dirty plaster
frontages embossed with scroll-work and heraldic devices. The whole district is like this: street leading   5
into street of houses like shabby monumental safes
crammed with the tarnished valuables and second-
hand furniture of a bankrupt middle class.

I am a camera with its shutter open, quite passive,
recording, not thinking. Recording the man shaving   10
at the window opposite and the woman in the
kimono washing her hair. Some day, all this will have
to be developed, carefully printed, fixed.

At eight o'clock in the evening the house-doors
will be locked. The children are having supper. The   15
shops are shut. The electric sign is switched on over
the night-bell of the little hotel on the corner, where
you can hire a room by the hour. And soon the
whistling will begin. Young men are calling their
girls. Standing down there in the cold, they whistle   20
up at the lighted windows of warm rooms where the
beds are already turned down for the night. They
want to be let in. Their signals echo down the deep
hollow street, lascivious and private and sad. Because
of the whistling, I do not care to stay here in the   25
evenings. It reminds me that I am in a foreign city,
alone, far from home. Sometimes I determine not to
listen to it, pick up a book, try to read. But soon a call
is sure to sound, so piercing, so insistent, so des-
pairingly human, that at last I have to get up and peep   30
through the slats of the Venetian blind to make quite

sure that it is not – as I know very well it could not
possibly be – for me.

The extraordinary smell in this room when the stove
is lighted and the window shut; not altogether un-   35
pleasant, a mixture of incense and stale buns. The tall
tiled stove, gorgeously coloured, like an altar. The
washstand like a Gothic shrine. The cupboard also is
Gothic, with carved cathedral windows: Bismarck
faces the King of Prussia in stained glass. My best   40
chair would do for a bishop's throne. In the corner,
three sham medieval halberds (from a theatrical
touring company?) are fastened together to form a
hatstand. Frl. Schroeder unscrews the heads of the
halberds and polishes them from time to time. They   45
are heavy and sharp enough to kill.
    Everything in the room is like that: unnecessarily
solid, abnormally heavy and dangerously sharp.
Here, at the writing-table, I am confronted by a
phalanx of metal objects – a pair of candlesticks   50
shaped like entwined serpents, an ashtray from which
emerges the head of a crocodile, a paperknife copied
from a Florentine dagger, a brass dolphin holding on
the end of its tail a small broken clock. What becomes
of such things? How could they ever be destroyed?   55
They will probably remain intact for thousands of
years: people will treasure them in museums. Or
perhaps they will merely be melted down for
munitions in a war. Every morning, Frl. Schroeder
arranges them very carefully in certain unvarying   60
positions: there they stand, like an uncompromising
statement of her views on Capital and Society, Religion and Sex.

(London: Minerva, 1989)

In his late twenties Isherwood spent four years in Berlin, and
Goodbye to Berlin, which he has called a 'roughly continuous narrative' and a 'loosely connected sequence of diaries and sketches',
covers that period in the early 1930s. He met up with other friends
and canonical 'thirties' writers such as W. H. Auden and Stephen
Spender who were similarly trying to escape the socially and espe-

cially sexually repressive atmosphere of England. At the time Berlin was seen as a place of licence and liberty, as is apparent in the opening pages of *Goodbye to Berlin* and in the plays that have been based on the novel: *I am a Camera* and *Cabaret*. Only as the 1930s develop does the atmosphere in the novel change from one of decadence to one of oppression alongside the rise of Hitler.

Isherwood arrived in Berlin in 1929, the year the Wall Street Crash seriously damaged all Western economies but devastated Germany's which had been severely hampered by reparations after the First World War. Democracy appeared to many to have failed, and the country faced a political dilemma: the communists or the fascists, both of whom achieved their best-ever result in the 1930 elections. In 1932, the Nazis polled 37 per cent in the Reichstag elections and in the following January Hitler was appointed German Chancellor. This is the period covered by Isherwood's novel, from Autumn 1930 to the early months of 1933.

The first of the six chapters is a light-hearted Berlin Diary set in Autumn 1930 and concerned with the narrator's personal life, while the Berlin Diary which closes the book is a doom-laden account of the public political world of Winter 1932–3 which Isherwood most clearly allegorises in a boxing match between Nazis and communists. Possibly to mimic the polarisation of the country, the middle four chapters also work as pairs: the first two, 'Sally Bowles' and 'On Ruegen Island', deal with sexual outlaws, the first heterosexual and the second homosexual, the next two, 'The Nowaks' and 'The Landauers', with social outlaws, the first an underprivileged working-class family and the second a prosperous Jewish family. Writing from the later 1930s, Isherwood knows that in Nazi Germany all these people will become 'The Lost', his original title for the novel which was to be a much longer collection of interconnected stories.

The opening three words, 'From my window', tell us that this is a first-person novel even though, by the use of incomplete sentences, the first 'I' does not appear until the second paragraph where the narrator tells us that 'I am a camera.' The opening paragraph has illustrated this as the narrator's eyes scan the view outside and passively record what they see (ll.9–10). However, many critics have questioned the plausibility of such uninvolved objectivity. Just as the narrator of this novel, the reader comes to realise, is called 'Christopher Isherwood' but is not to be equated with the author, descriptive language is never as impersonal as a quietly recording film, leaving aside the fact that both fiction and film rely on selection, angles and editing. Isherwood's choice of terms such as 'deep solemn massive street' (l.1) and images such as 'houses like shabby monumental safes' (l.6) requires us to take lightly the documentary claims of passive observation. For example, the simile of houses like safes 'crammed with the tarnished valuables and second-hand furniture of a bankrupt middle class' (ll.7–8) is a carefully chosen image suggesting Germany's fallen grandeur, caused by reparation payments, the stock market crash, political turmoil and unprecedented inflation rises. This is underlined when Isherwood's camera moves inside his lodgings a few paragraphs later and portrays the impoverished Frl. Schroeder's house as a museum stockpiled with grandiose antiques (ll.34–44). Also, the qualifiers in the opening paragraph illustrate a particular understanding of the world outside the narrator's window: lamps burn 'under the shadow', balcony façades are 'top-heavy', plaster frontages are 'dirty' (ll.2–4). While these details are all 'factual' they are selective and connected to create a pejorative impression. The narrator as he stares out of the window considers himself to *be* a camera, not just *like* one, because he is 'not thinking' (l.10), but by the time Isherwood comes to write the first sentences of the novel he is ordering, organising, arranging.

The use of the present tense is a noticeable feature of the opening. Most of the story will be written in the past tense but the opening and closing diaries are begun with a direct address to the reader through the pages of Isherwood's journal. To transpose such observations into the past they will have to be 'developed, carefully printed, fixed' (l.13). Isherwood's claim to be an objective recorder is strengthened, however, by his outsider status, by the fact that he is 'in a foreign city, alone, far from home' (ll.26–7). It is also a stance skilfully insinuated by the very first sentence which, like others later in the opening, has no subject (or verb). The 'I' which does not appear until the second paragraph ought to complete the opening line: 'From my window, [I look at] the deep solemn massive street'. As the incomplete sentence stands it suggests that the street simply *is* there, objectively fixed but not subjectively viewed. The second sentence similarly lacks both subject and verb, amounting only to a list of descriptors and nouns (also see Isherwood's first sentences about his room beginning on line 34). Such techniques serve to erase the presence of the narrator, just as, Isherwood once said, the narrator has the same name as the author to deter the reader from thinking of him as a character in his own right (the author Isherwood called the narrator Isherwood a demi-character). This is underlined in the third paragraph when the narrator talks of the street life from which he is excluded. He can see into the rooms, and in a sense the lives, of people in other buildings, and he can hear the sounds of the street, the calls of lovers which, since he is alone in his room, alienate him further since they are calls that 'could not possibly be – for me' (ll.32–3). The 'calling' (l.19), 'whistling' (l.25) and 'signals' (l.23) also remind the reader of the clandestine world of Berlin as it enters the 1930s: of the coming organised Nazi night raids on Jewish stores, of the distorted shadows of people running down threatening 'hollow street[s]' (l.24). This is the world that will be described in the later sections of the novel whose atmosphere will become increasingly expressionistic in its use of violent imagery, dark and shadows, projected fears and mounting paranoia. The fact that Isherwood feels compelled to go and 'peep' to see if the boys whistling for their lovers are trying to attract his attention also reminds the reader of the chief personal reason why several writers such as Auden and Isherwood went to Berlin in the first place: for homosexual experience (this could also be linked to Isherwood's knowledge that the hotel opposite rents rooms by the hour: ll. 17–18).

After the line break, the narrator's camera turns inside to his own room and lodging house. After the opening page's complete concentration on sight and sound, the appropriate two kinds of sensory perception for a 'camera', this fourth paragraph begins with the sense of smell. The paragraph introduces the theme of violence which will lurk in the background of the stories until the final Berlin Diary. Isherwood does this here through his description of the furniture, particularly the hatstand composed of 'three sham medieval halberds' (l.42) which are 'sharp enough to kill' (l.46). These anticipate the second Diary's Nazi banners which have staves with 'sharp metal points, shaped into arrow-heads' (p.247).

Isherwood's Berlin is a city of dangerous objects waiting for the Nazis. His room has 'a phalanx of metal objects' (l.50) that are 'unnecessarily solid, abnormally heavy and dangerously sharp' (l.48). (Later, at the very start of Part 4 of the novel, the narrator even says that at the end of one street 'like a tall, dangerously sharp red instrument, stood a church'.) This final paragraph also makes reference to another important set of metaphors through its animal imagery, reminiscent of Eugène Ionesco's absurdist play *Rhinoceros* (1960) in which actors literally don the heads of pachyderms to indicate that their characters have gone over to the fascists. The suggestion that Berlin will lose its humanity is there in the objects surrounding the narrator in his room where there is mention of candlestick 'serpents' (l.51), an ashtray 'crocodile' (l.52) and a clock in the tail of a 'dolphin' (l.53). Even these things will perhaps 'be melted down for munitions in a war' (l.58). The ornaments are carefully arranged, unchanging, and 'will probably remain intact for thousands of years' (l.56). These objects belong to the first major character encountered in the novel, the landlady Frl. Schroeder, and they stand 'like an uncompromising statement on her views on Capital and Society, Religion and Sex' (ll. 61–3). To express the force of Frl. Schroeder's views, Isherwood accords the four words capital letters, making them as heavy and serious as both Frl. Schroeder's possessions and her opinions. Isherwood once described her as symbolic of the whole German public, because she is well-meaning but unwary, but also because she will always be there, like her ordinary but potentially sinister possessions; while the Third Reich may come and go, the ordinary German people will persist.

The reverential stained glass pictures of Bismarck and the King of Prussia (ll. 39–40) imply that Frl. Schroeder looks to the strong Prussian leaders of the past, and her admiration for Bismarck (1815–98), the Iron Chancellor who unified the country, expanded the empire, provoked war with France and reorganised Germany under the leadership of Prussia, suggests that she will also be susceptible to the strong leadership of Hitler.

The room is also strongly associated with, first, the past (items are associated with the 'medieval' (l.42) and the 'Gothic' (l.38), and might later transfer to 'museums': l.57) and, second, a church (note the references to 'incense' (l.36), 'altar' (l.37), 'shrine' (l.38), 'cathedral windows' (l.39), and 'bishop's throne': l.41). It is for this reason the objects seem to stand as statements on Frl. Schroeder's opinions about Capital (the associations with treasure (l.57) and the past), Society (the violent aspect), Religion (church imagery) and Sex (the animal figures).

Ultimately, however, all the major characters in the novel are seen as victims of the rise of fascism in the country. Each one is persecuted for some aspect of their lives, to do with class, sexuality, money, nationality, religion or politics, which is why the novel has to be a farewell to the city, for both Isherwood and for the Germany that existed before Hitler's (ir)resistible rise to power.

Further Reading

Finney, Brian (1981) *Christopher Isherwood: A Critical Biography*, London: Faber & Faber.

Hynes, Samuel (1972) *The Auden Generation*, London: Faber & Faber.

Piazza, Paul (1978) *Christopher Isherwood: Myth and Anti-Myth*, New York: Columbia University Press.

Wade, Stephen (1992) *Christopher Isherwood*, London: Macmillan – now Palgrave.

Malcolm Lowry
Under the Volcano
(1947)

Two mountain chains traverse the republic roughly from north
to south, forming between them a number of valleys and pla-
teaux. Overlooking one of these valleys, which is dominated by
two volcanoes, lies, six thousand feet above sea-level, the town of
Quauhnahuac. It is situated well south of the Tropic of Cancer,   5
to be exact, on the nineteenth parallel, in about the same latitude
as the Revillagigedo Islands to the west in the Pacific, or very
much farther west, the southernmost tip of Hawaii – and as the
port of Tzucox to the east on the Adriatic seaboard of Yucatan
near the border of British Honduras, or very much farther east,   10
the town of Juggernaut, in India, in the Bay of Bengal.
    The walls of the town, which is built on a hill, are high, the
streets and lanes tortuous and broken, the roads winding. A fine
American-style highway leads in from the north but is lost in its
narrow streets and comes out a goat track. Quauhnahuac posses-   15
ses eighteen churches and fifty-seven *cantinas*. It also boasts a
golf course and no fewer than four hundred swimming-pools,
public and private, filled with the water that ceaselessly pours
down from the mountains, and many splendid hotels.
    The Hotel Casino de la Selva stands on a slightly higher hill   20
just outside the town, near the railway station. It is built far
back from the main highway and surrounded by gardens and
terraces which command a spacious view in every direction.
Palatial, a certain air of desolate splendour pervades it. For it is
no longer a Casino. You may not even dice for drinks in the   25
bar. The ghosts of ruined gamblers haunt it. No one ever seems
to swim in the magnificent Olympic pool. The springboards
stand empty and mournful. Its jai-alai courts are grass-grown
and deserted. Two tennis courts only are kept up in the sea-
son.   30
    Towards sunset on the Day of the Dead in November 1939,

two men in white flannels sat on the main terrace of the Casino
drinking *anís*. They had been playing tennis, followed by billi-
ards, and their rackets, rainproofed, screwed in their presses –
the doctor's triangular, the other's quadrangular – lay on the   35
parapet before them. As the processions winding from the
cemetery down the hillside behind the hotel came closer the
plangent sounds of their chanting were borne to the two men;
they turned to watch the mourners, a little later to be visible
only as the melancholy lights of their candles, circling among   40
the distant trussed cornstalks. Dr Arturo Díaz Vigil pushed the
bottle of Anís del Mono over to M. Jacques Laruelle, who now
was leaning forward intently.

Slightly to the right and below them, below the gigantic red
evening, whose reflection bled away in the deserted swimming   45
pools scattered everywhere like so many mirages, lay the peace
and sweetness of the town. It seemed peaceful enough from
where they were sitting. Only if one listened intently, as M.
Laruelle was doing now, could one distinguish a remote confused sound – distinct yet somehow inseparable from the mi-   50
nute murmuring, the tintinnabulation of the mourners – as of
singing, rising, and falling, and a steady trampling – the bangs
and cries of the *fiesta* that had been going on all day.

M. Laruelle poured himself another *anís*. He was drinking
anís because it reminded him of absinthe. A deep flush had suf-   55
fused his face, and his hand trembled slightly over the bottle,
from whose label a florid demon brandished a pitchfork at him.

(Harmondsworth: Penguin, 1962)

In 1936, the peripatetic Lowry settled in the resort town of
Cuernavaca, some 50 miles south of Mexico City, where he soon
began writing his masterpiece, initially as a short story. *Under the
Volcano* would take ten years to revise fully as Lowry added layer
upon layer of mythological reference, mystical symbolism and literary allusion. After the first chapter, the novel chronicles the final
twelve hours in the life of a British ex-consul in Quauhnahuac, the
Indian name for the town of Cuernavaca. Though most frequently
focalised through the mind of the Consul, the book presents the story
through the eyes of other characters in some chapters, and its first
chapter is set exactly one year in the future, after the Consul's death.
The novel develops as a phantasmagoric late modernist *tour de force*
which follows the day-in-the-life approach of Joyce's *Ulysses* and

Woolf's *Mrs Dalloway*, but draws on Lowry's personal interests in Romanticism, expressionism, symbolism and the cabbala. In conventional terms little happens, as the Consul embarks on a drinking spree, while his wife, who has temporarily returned to him, and his brother, who has been fighing in Spain, try to keep him from harm, whether inflicted by himself or by the corrupt Mexican police, who do shoot him at the novel's close. The book's fascination lies in its exemplary use of modernist devices: baroque symbolism, rococo imagery, interior monologue, mythological allusion, defamiliarisation, time-shifting, fast-cutting, and intensely resonant, rhythmical, poetic prose. Like Joyce's *Ulysses* it is a book about everything: politics, history, Western literature, religion, psychology and human relationships. To this day, the single best way to approach the novel is undoubtedly through Lowry's 35-page 1946 letter (reprinted in the 1985 Penguin edition) to his British publisher, Jonathan Cape, detailing and defending the book's dense construction and intricate organisation.

Under the Volcano is one of the most complex of twentieth-century novels, but its opening is deceptively simple. It begins almost in the style of a travel brochure with a report of the area surrounding Quauhnahuac and of its position in the world (the mountain chains running north and south describe Quauhnahuac's position in terms of longitude and the nineteenth parallel pinpoints the town's latitude). The narrative then moves to the Mexican town itself before settling on the Hotel Casino de la Selva. Only after this spatial orientation, which has worked like a camera zooming in on the hotel, does the fourth paragraph shift from present to past tense and introduce the date and time of the story. It is the end, the demise, of the Day of the Dead, 2 November 1939 (l.31): a day on which the dead are thought to commune with the living.

The details of the opening paragraph appear random, chosen from the accidents of the political map, yet each place mentioned by the narrator has a significance to the story: for example, India (l.11), which is 'very much farther east', was where the Consul's mother died and his father deserted him, while Hawaii (l.8), which is 'very much farther west', was the place where the Consul's wife, Yvonne, grew up (a place also famous for its volcanoes). Much in this beginning symbolises the couple: the 'Two mountain chains' (l.1) and the 'two volcanoes' (l.4): Popocatepetl, the volcano of the title, and Popo's 'wife' Ixtaccihuatl, the Sleeping Woman.

Similarly, the details of the second paragraph are important, even though they appear to be banal facts listed as though for tourists.

The description enumerates only churches and *cantinas*, together with a golf course and 400 swimming pools. The reason for this is that this is to be, in the simplest of terms, a novel about a drunk who seeks but will not ask for God's salvation. The Consul's earliest significant experiences centre on a golf course in north-west England and the pools represent baptism and spiritual renewal, as in T. S. Eliot's *The Waste Land*, which is apparent later in the novel when the narrator asks of the Consul's swimming-pool: '*Might a soul bathe there and be clean or slake its drought?*' (p.78). Nobody even swims in the 'magnificent Olympic pool' whose springboards 'stand empty and mournful', suiting both the Day of the Dead and also this first anniversary of the Consul's death. It is into these deserted pools that the red evening's reflection will be found later to have 'bled away' (l.45). That Quauhnahuac is a doomed town is suggested by the highway which dwindles down to become a 'goat track' (l.15), while the town's own streets are 'tortuous and broken', its roads 'winding' (l.13).

By the third paragraph the reader should also have gained an almost oppressive impression of height from the various descriptions. At the start we are introduced to the Sierra Madre mountains and to volcanoes, plus a town 'six thousand feet above sea level' (l.4). The town, 'which is built on a hill' (l.12) has walls that are 'high' (l.12), and the 'terraced' Hotel Casino de la Selva is on a 'slightly higher hill' again (l.20). Together, the descriptions create a sense of a towering landscape which will dwarf the novel's protagonists, and this is also one of the resonances of the book's title (the theme of the Fall, central to the novel, is also suggested). The mood of decay which runs through the rest of the paragraph initiates the sense of loss that will characterise this opening chapter, which is set in the future after the death of the Consul and his wife, and two months after the start of the Second World War, thus creating the impression that this is a dilapidated, God-forsaken world which has gone to seed. Like the opening of *A Passage to India*, which is also cinematic, this beginning has many negatives, with a Casino that is 'no longer a Casino' (l.25), 'deserted' jai-alai courts (l.28) and 'a certain air of desolate splendour' (l.24). That the town is 'surrounded by gardens' is important because one of the main themes of the novel is the Consul's fall from grace presented in terms of Adam and Eve's eviction from Eden. The final lines of the novel, which have been quoted several times earlier, are: ¿LE GUSTA ESTE JARDIN? ¿QUE ES SUYO? ¡EVITE QUE SUS HIJOS LO DESTRUYAN! The sentences, which mean 'Do you like this garden? Is it yours? Do not let your children destroy it!', are mistranslated by the Consul as 'You like this garden? Why is it yours? We evict those who destroy!' For the Consul, the gardens and terraces of Quauhnahuac, in which he is tormented, prompt him to reinterpret the 'old legend of the Garden of Eden': '"What if Adam wasn't really banished from the place at all? ... What if his punishment really consisted", the consul continued with warmth, "in his having to *go on living there*, alone, of course – suffering, unseen, cut off from God"' (p.137).

The fourth paragraph introduces the chapter's two main characters, M. Laruelle and Dr Vigil, who turn to watch the chanting Day of the Dead mourners spiralling down the hillside like Virgil wandering down the circles of Dante's hell. It is M. Laruelle's last day in Mexico, and it is he who years ago had a pivotal affair with the Consul's wife and through whom this first chapter will be focalised. Laruelle is a filmmaker and the cinematic opening alludes to this: indeed Lowry suggested that the novel after Chapter 1 could be seen as Laruelle's film of the Consul's life. While Laruelle is an old friend of the Consul's, from his days in Leasowe, Dr Vigil is a new one who, as his name suggests, kept watch over the Consul (as the mourners have kept a vigil overnight since the previous All Saints Day). Together they represent the good and bad angels who have sat on the Consul's shoulders and bargained for his soul. The fifth paragraph turns to the positive aspect of the Day, in the confused sounds of the *fiesta*, through which Lowry creates the peculiar mood on All Souls Day in Mexico when death is simultaneously lamented and celebrated just as the 'minute murmuring' of the mourners merges with the 'bangs and cries' of the festival (ll.50–3).

The final paragraph turns to the subject of drink, with which the rest of the novel will also be concerned. M. Laruelle's face flushes and his hand shakes, images which will remind the familiar reader of the Consul, of whom Dr Vigil is about to speak. Finally, and appropriately for a novel which Lowry intended as the alcoholic Faustian 'hell' of a projected modern Divine Comedy, this passage ends with a bottle of *anís* whose label depicts 'a florid demon' threatening with a pitchfork.

Reviewing the passage, we can identify its chief connections with the remainder of the novel and its themes: the references to alcohol, the 'ghosts' (l.26) that haunt the town, the mourners circling down the hill on the anniversary of the Consul and Yvonne's death, and the allusions to the scene of Yvonne's death, a wood, in the name of the Hotel – *selva* means wood – and that of the town itself which, Laruelle says to Yvonne, means 'near the wood' (p.49) and not

'Where the eagle stops!' (she releases a caged eagle in the wood: p.320). The introduction of the 'wood' is also meant as a reference to Dante's *Inferno*, which begins in 'a dark wood', and the strains of this connection are present in details like the play on Vigil/Virgil, the 'demon' label, and the way that the evening is said to have 'bled' away, as though dying. In the crevices of this introductory page and a half there are allusions and portents in every line, the accumulation of which over the course of the novel create in the reader the ominous sense of a modern tragedy played out in language and symbols appropriate to a world poised between the betrayals of the Spanish Civil War and the horrors of the new world war only just beginning.

Further Reading

Bareham, Tony (1989) *Malcolm Lowry*, London: Macmillan – now Palgrave.
Day, Douglas (1973) *Malcolm Lowry*, Oxford: Oxford University Press.
Lowry, Malcolm (1995) *Sursum Corda! The Collected Letters of Malcolm Lowry*, vol. 1: 1926–46 (ed. Sherrill E. Grace), London: Jonathan Cape.
Smith, Anne (ed.) (1978) *The Art of Malcolm Lowry*, London: Vision.

Jean Rhys
Wide Sargasso Sea
(1966)

They say when trouble comes close ranks, and so the white people
did. But we were not in their ranks. The Jamaican ladies had never
approved of my mother, 'because she pretty like pretty self'
Christophine said.

She was my father's second wife, far too young for him they   5
thought, and, worse still, a Martinique girl. When I asked her why
so few people came to see us, she told me that the road from Spanish
Town to Coulibri Estate where we lived was very bad and that road
repairing was now a thing of the past. (My father, visitors, horses,
feeling safe in bed – all belonged to the past.)   10

Another day I heard her talking to Mr Luttrell, our neighbour and
her only friend. 'Of course they have their own misfortunes. Still
waiting for this compensation the English promised when the Emancipation Act was passed. Some wait for a long time.'

How could she know that Mr Luttrell would be the first who grew 15
tired of waiting? One calm evening he shot his dog, swam out to sea
and was gone for always. No agent came from England to look after
his property – Nelson's Rest it was called – and strangers from
Spanish Town rode up to gossip and discuss the tragedy.

'Live at Nelson's Rest? Not for love or money. An unlucky place.'   20

Mr Luttrell's house was left empty, shutters banging in the wind.
Soon the black people said it was haunted, they wouldn't go near it.
And no one came near us.

I got used to a solitary life, but my mother still planned and hoped
– perhaps she had to hope every time she passed a looking glass.   25

She still rode about every morning not caring that the black people
stood about in groups to jeer at her, especially after her riding clothes
grew shabby (they notice clothes, they know about money).

Then one day, very early, I saw her horse lying down under the
frangipani tree. I went up to him but he was not sick, he was dead   30
and his eyes were black with flies. I ran away and did not speak of it

for I thought if I told no one it might not be true. But later that day,
Godfrey found him, he had been poisoned. 'Now we are marooned,'
my mother said, 'now what will become of us?'

Godfrey said, 'I can't watch the horse night and day. I too old now. 35
When the old time go, let it go. No use to grab at it. The Lord make
no distinction between black and white, black and white the same for
Him. Rest yourself in peace for the righteous are not forsaken.' But
she couldn't. She was young. How could she not try for all the things
that had gone so suddenly, so without warning. 'You're blind when   40
you want to be blind,' she said ferociously, 'and you're deaf when you
want to be deaf. The old hypocrite,' she kept saying. 'He knew what
they were going to do.' 'The devil prince of this world,' Godfrey
said, 'but this world don't last so long for mortal man.'

(Harmondsworth: Penguin, 1997)

Wide Sargasso Sea is divided into three parts. Although other secondary narrators appear, the first part is narrated by Antoinette Cosway, the second by an unnamed man whom she marries, and the third by Antoinette again. It soon becomes clear to the reader that these two narrators will be more familiar to anyone who has read *Jane Eyre* as Rochester and Bertha Mason, his first 'mad' wife. Rhys's novel has therefore been called a 'prequel' to *Jane Eyre* but this should not be taken literally as there are differences, not least of chronology, between them that mean the characters in the two novels cannot be simply equated. Most of *Jane Eyre* takes place in the first decade of the century but *Wide Sargasso Sea* crucially begins with the end of slavery: 'Still waiting for this compensation the English promised when the Emancipation Act was passed' (ll.12–14), which was in 1833. Slavery was legally abolished on 1 August 1834, the year that Antoinette's father dies. In many history books this legislation is portrayed as a great humanitarian move on the part of the British, in contrast with the rest of Europe, but fear of rebellion was a major factor. The Jamaican uprising of 1831–2 was perhaps decisive at a time when widespread unrest across the West Indies was feared and so *Wide Sargasso Sea*'s opening on Jamaica is partly important precisely because it was the site of intensive black resistance.

Each part of the novel is set on a different island, in a different country (Jamaica, Dominica and England respectively). The shift in location provides a shift in narrator, and each time this serves to underline a different kind of homelessness. In the first section, Antoinette narrates the story of the burning of her house and her move to the alienating environment of the convent in a series of events that would seem to be in imitation of what happens to Jane Eyre: Antoinette is made an orphan, has to stay with relatives, and gets sent to a special school. *Wide Sargasso Sea* opens, like *Jane Eyre*, with a first-person conversational narrative that begins with an impersonal statement: the narrator does not introduce herself to the reader, and so Rhys's novel should not be considered to be modelled on an autobiography in the way that *Robinson Crusoe* or *Great Expectations* could arguably be said to be. The narrator appears to be recounting details about her life but she makes no attempt to 'begin at the beginning' of her life in any sense, and this approach is replicated at the start of the second part when 'Rochester' commences his story with the words 'So it was all over', as though he were picking up where he, or Antoinette, had left off a previous narrative. Antoinette tells us nothing about herself in these opening pages but she tells us many things about her family and society. The 'gossip' that Antoinette talks about also seems to characterise her own anecdotal style which conforms more to features of oral narratives than written ones. This impression is intensified by the use of creole patois expressions like 'she pretty like pretty self' (l.3).

Antoinette, an adolescent of 13 when the novel opens, immediately establishes a situation in which she and her family are positioned between other groups, most obviously between 'the white people' (l.1) and 'the black people' (l.22); an impression exacerbated by the use of the army term 'ranks' (l.2). Though she reports many things said by individuals she is close to, she also gives a collective identity to other people and to sayings, as with the phrases 'They say' (l.1) and 'the Jamaican ladies' (l.2) in the first lines, or the quotation apparently attributed simply to 'strangers' in line 20. The opening suggests that Antoinette does not consider herself important to her own story. The worst aspect to her life for Antoinette is that she does not belong anywhere. Rochester's changing of her name to Bertha also signals this losing or stealing of her identity.

The title of the novel can be considered to symbolise the wide gap between Antoinette and Rochester particularly, but the separation between Antoinette as a creole and both whites and blacks in general. The principal image in the novel of this in-between life is the figure of the zombie (for instance, Rochester says 'A zombi is a dead person who seems to be alive or a living person who is dead'), and the internal numbness and despair that Antoinette experiences suggests that she feels she is not one of the 'righteous who are not forsaken' (l.38) but 'marooned' (l.33) between life and death (the descendants of runaway slaves, the number of whom had greatly increased in the 1820s, were known as 'maroons' in Jamaica). The link to the religion of voodoo, from which the idea of the zombie comes, is made through Christophine, a woman who was 'given' as a wedding-present from Antoinette's father to her mother. Christophine comes from another island in the Windwards, Martinique (1.6), which was a French colony like Haiti (Antoinette's mother was also from Martinique). One of the importances of Martinique in the novel is its association with *obeah*, a weak form of voodoo, the African religion which was most prevalent on Haiti. Rhys writes in her letters that 'From the start it must be made clear that Christophine is an *obeah* woman.' *Obeah* is opposed in the novel to Christianity, which is referred to at the start in Godfrey's assertion that 'The Lord make no distinction between black and white' (ll.36–7). Yet, at this opening, Godfrey also warns that it is not God but the devil who is, in a Biblical reference, 'prince of this world' (1.43), and the suggestion is that while 'this world don't last so long for mortal man' (1.44), it will for those caught between life and death: real or metaphorical 'zombies'.

Rhys's original title for the novel was '*le revenant*' (the returner), a mixed reference to zombies and to the novel's revisiting of *Jane Eyre*. It is also the name by which Martinique is known: '*le pays des revenants*', 'the country of those who come back'. Titles were very important to Rhys and she had at one stage rejected the title *Wide Sargasso Sea* because few people would know what it meant (her letters however say that it comes from a creole song written by a cousin of hers). The sea is named after the floating brown seaweed that abounds in it called *sargassam natans*. Ships travelling across the sea would have to negotiate these weeds which could leave them entangled and *marooned*. The image is then of both a stretch of water between the West Indies and Europe, and of tendrils that can ensnarl. Critics take this in three ways: as a metaphor for slavery, or for women's position in the nineteenth century, or for the position of Antoinette and Rochester – bound together.

Born on Dominica, one of the Windward Islands, Jean Rhys was herself a white creole, like Antoinette. 'Creole' is a term often applied to whites born in the Caribbean, but it has also referred to blacks born there. Its common meanings have been, first, 'born of mixed parentage', and second, 'immigrants from Europe'. Its primary significance for the novel is to indicate Antoinette's position as an outsider. *Wide Sargasso Sea* has two Caribbean locations. The first part is set in Jamaica; the second part is set, critics believe, on Dominica.

Though Jamica was independent (from 1962) at the time *Wide Sargasso Sea* was published in 1966, Dominica was not. Dominica became self-governing in 1967, and an independent country within the British commonwealth in 1978. Written therefore at the time of the independence movement in the Caribbean, *Wide Sargasso Sea* has the history of slavery hanging over it: Antoinette's mother is the daughter and the widow of a slave-owner, and the first town mentioned in the novel is Spanish Town, the capital of Jamaica at this time, containing one of the Caribbean's major slave markets. Before the 1830s the British Caribbean was a single-crop slave economy producing sugar for export with no attention given to local needs. Tobacco, cotton, ginger, cocoa and coffee were also grown but the 'white gold' as sugar was known, was the primary export after the middle of the seventeenth century (Rhys toyed with calling the book 'Gold Sargasso Sea'). It has been estimated that money from this trade brought at the start of the eighteenth century the greatest increase in British wealth in modern times. For this economy, credit was needed – and provided by English bankers – and so was labour. There was little local labour (the indigenous peoples, the Caribs and the Arawaks having been wiped out) and so the African slave trade began. On the gold coast in West Africa, English products such as textiles, cutlery, brass and copper goods were exchanged for human beings who were then taken to the Americas and sold for money that was returned to London: hence the term 'triangular slave trade'. Up to the 1830s, the time of *Wide Sargasso Sea*, Britain had made about £450 million from its triangular trade and about £150 million from the West Indian sugar trade. But, for Antoinette's family, the 1830s are a time of decline, they are creoles caught between blacks and whites, ostracised by both ethnic groups and, because they are isolated, 'when trouble comes' they are unable to 'close ranks' (1.1). For this reason the novel begins with an image of the family caught in the middle like ships in the *sargassam natans*, marooned from others and from their previous prosperity: 'no one came near us' (1.23). Amid the images of dead horses, and empty houses, in Antoinette's 'solitary life' (1.24) everything has 'gone for always' (1.17) and she and her family are simply cut off: 'road repairing was now a thing of the past. (My father, visitors, horses, feeling safe in bed – all belonged to the past.)' (ll.8–10).

Postscript: *Jane Eyre* and *Wide Sargasso Sea*

Edward Said tells a salutary story about reading in a student essay that Charlotte Brontë must have read *Wide Sargasso Sea*. While it is absurd to suggest this could have happened, it is not absurd to see *Jane Eyre* as posterior to *Wide Sargasso Sea* from the perspective of the reader. In fact reading *Wide Sargasso Sea* before *Jane Eyre* is probably now in many ways helpful in considering the earlier novel from a postcolonial point of view. The influence of Rhys on Brontë criticism – in the sense of the way *Jane Eyre* is now often analysed – is in fact very large. In this respect, it is Gayatri Spivak's reading that has most popularised postcolonial readings of *Jane Eyre* but it is *Wide Sargasso Sea* that has changed the reading paradigm associated with Brontë's novel. No longer is *Jane Eyre* seen as a text possessing a heroine with which the reader identifies but one which is historically placed. In Rhys's novel the character Jane Eyre occupies as little of the text as Bertha Mason does in Brontë's novel. Rhys is also careful to give Antoinette a similar upbringing to Jane Eyre's: orphanhood, poverty, social humiliation, repressive schooling, lack of love. Rhys makes Brontë's novel dependent upon hers by writing a *pre-text*, and in so doing mirrors the dependence of England on its Empire. Several colonial factors are significant here: slavery and indentured labour are echoed in Rochester's contractural buying of Antoinette; the substitution of an Anglicised name, Bertha, for Antoinette's original one mirrors the imposition of English on the colonies. 'Bertha' is also transported overseas, like a slave, and forcibly imprisoned. And lastly Rochester's name is never mentioned in *Wide Sargasso Sea* as though to mirror the impersonality of the colonial encounter (the dehumanisation of both coloniser and colonised).

This leaves the question of to what degree is *Wide Sargasso Sea* consonant with a postcolonial perspective? Judie Newman, for example, says that for all the book's revisionings it remains the story of a white slave-owner's daughter. *Wide Sargasso Sea* contains stories of omens, zombies, *obeah* and poisons substituted for Brontë's depiction of a foul crazed animal.

In conclusion, Antoinette and Rochester are shown as culturally incompatible. She paints roses at the convent which are never red: instead, they are purple, blue and green. He feels that the landscape he sees is 'too much': 'too much blue, too much purple, too much green'. Even the trees are threatening to him. The novel also expresses a fear of colonial female sexuality. All sexual desire is called a thirst in the novel. Antoinette's sexual desire is considered by Rochester an index of her racial contamination. Initially aroused by her sexual desire he is repelled when he finds he is not its only object. Rochester's attempt and wish to control Antoinette thus mirrors the colonial desire to 'civilise' the West Indies. For all that the act represents in *Jane Eyre*, burning down Thornfield at the end of *Wide Sargasso Sea* burns down all the partitions in Antoinette's head: between herself and Christophine or her childhood friend Tia, between England (grey) and Jamaica (colourful like the frangipani tree: 1.30), between white and black, colonised and coloniser.

Further Reading

Davidson, Arnold E. (1985) *Jean Rhys*, New York: Frederick Ungar.

Horner, Avril and Zlosnik, Sue (1990) *Landscapes of Desire*, Hemel Hempstead: Harvester.

Hulme, Peter (1994) 'The Locked Heart: the creole family romance of *Wide Sargasso Sea*' in *Colonial Discourse/Postcolonial Theory* (ed. F. Barker, P. Hulme and M. Iversen), Manchester: Manchester University Press.

Newman, Judie (1995) *The Ballistic Bard*, London: Edward Arnold.

Angela Carter
The Bloody Chamber
(1979)

I remember how, that night, I lay awake in the wagon-lit in a tender, delicious ecstasy of excitement, my burning cheek pressed against the impeccable linen of the pillow and the pounding of my heart mimicking that of the great pistons ceaselessly thrusting the train that bore me through the night, away from Paris, away from girlhood, away from the 5 white, enclosed quietude of my mother's apartment, into the unguess-able country of marriage.

And I remember I tenderly imagined how, at this very moment, my mother would be moving slowly about the narrow bedroom I had left behind for ever, folding up and putting away all my little relics, the 10 tumbled garments I would not need anymore, the scores for which there had been no room in my trunks, the concert programmes I'd abandoned; she would linger over this torn ribbon and that faded photograph with all the half-joyous, half-sorrowful emotions of a woman on her daughter's wedding-day. And, in the midst of my bridal 15 triumph, I felt a pang of loss as if, when he put the gold band on my finger, I had, in some way, ceased to be her child in becoming his wife.

Are you sure, she'd said when they delivered the gigantic box that held the wedding dress he'd bought me, wrapped up in tissue paper and red ribbon like a Christmas gift of crystallized fruit. Are you sure 20 you love him? There was a dress for her, too; black silk, with the dull, prismatic sheen of oil on water, finer than anything she'd worn since that adventurous girlhood in Indo-China, daughter of a rich tea planter. My eagle-featured, indomitable mother; what other student at the Conservatoire could boast that her mother had outfaced a junkful of 25 Chinese pirates, nursed a village through a visitation of the plague, shot a man-eating tiger with her own hand and all before she was as old as I?

'Are you sure you love him?'

'I'm sure I want to marry him,' I said. 30

And would say no more. She sighed, as if it was with reluctance that

she might at last banish the spectre of poverty from its habitual place
at our meagre table. For my mother herself had gladly, scandalously,
defiantly beggared herself for love; and, one fine day, her gallant
soldier never returned from the wars, leaving his wife and child a   35
legacy of tears that never quite dried, a cigar box full of medals and the
antique service revolver that my mother, grown magnificently eccentric
in hardship, kept always in her reticule, in case – how I teased her –
she was surprised by footpads on her way home from the grocer's shop.

    Now and then a starburst of lights spattered the drawn blinds as if   40
the railway company had lit up all the stations through which we
passed in celebration of the bride. My satin nightdress had just been
shaken from its wrappings; it had slipped over my young girl's pointed
breasts and shoulders, supple as a garment of heavy water, and now
teasingly caressed me, egregious, insinuating, nudging between my   45
thighs as I shifted restlessly in my narrow berth. His kiss, his kiss with
tongue and teeth in it and a rasp of beard, had hinted to me, though
with the same exquisite tact as this nightdress he'd given me, of the
wedding night, which would be voluptuously deferred until we lay in
his great ancestral bed in the sea-girt, pinnacled domain that lay, still,   50
beyond the grasp of my imagination ... That magic place, the fairy
castle whose walls were made of foam, that legendary habitation in
which he had been born. To which, one day, I might bear an heir. Our
destination, my destiny.

(London: Picador, 1979)

The source for Angela Carter's short story is hinted at in the phrase
'rasp of beard' (l.47): 'The Bloody Chamber' is based on Charles
Perrault's fairy story of Bluebeard. Carter is aware of the different
versions of the story and its possible basis in real life (see Duncker,
1986: 232–3). Her story also plays with a number of other fairy tales,
such as Rapunzel, Cinderella and Red Riding Hood (for example,
note 'the antique service revolver that my mother, ... kept always in
her reticule, in case ... she was surprised by footpads on her way
home from the grocer's shop': ll.36–9). But Carter also parodies
various literary genres, such as gothic (in the remote castle with its
dungeon) and romance (in the rescue on a white charger and the
rags to riches story involving music, money and marriage), as well as
the narratives of religion and opera. She also toys with the conventions of realism. 'The Bloody Chamber' begins with the stock characters of a beggared-for-love widow, 'daughter of a rich tea-planter'
(l.23), and her only daughter, who appears an icon of Victorian duty

and respectability, living humbly in an apartment in Paris. Carter complicates this stereotype by making the unnamed narrator's mother a kind of adventure hero who has shot tigers and fought Chinese pirates. Immediately, the story incorporates incongruity to make the reader think about the conventions of certain kinds of narrative, and Carter includes some interesting oddities in the story that mirror the way in which she blends genres. The impoverished lifestyle of the 17-year-old narrator includes a maid, and thus simultaneously evokes the 'charm' of poverty and the 'allure' of wealth. The world of castles and white horses is mixed up with telephone calls from agents in New York, uniting Romantic chivalry and high-tech modern lifestyles. Overall, the story seems to attempt to tantalise the reader with every form of narrative pleasure: horror, romance, pornography, adventure story and fairy tale. Also, the exaggerated use of rich description ('from the white, enclosed quietude of my mother's apartment: ll.5–6) and the overblown language (e.g. 'into the unguessable country of marriage': ll.6–7) draws attention to the artificiality and conventionality of the narrative process.

Carter's story additionally has intertextual allusions to such canonical nineteenth-century poems as Browning's 'My Last Duchess' and Tennyson's 'The Lady of Shalott'. At one level, 'The Bloody Chamber' is clearly concerned with the re-working of 'legendary' (1.52) male discourses centred on fainting heroines rescued by 'gallant' (1.34) knights in shining armour. In this it juxtaposes the Medieval Romance with the Mills and Boon romance. More important is the element of rewritten fairy tales, a project which seems to develop from Carter's translations of Perrault's fairy tales in 1977. According to Patricia Duncker fairy tales arise from two main traditions: the first is the German *Märchen* (derived from the word for news or gossip) and *Volksmärchen* (meaning 'folk' tale); the second are those oral tales appropriated by the French aristocratic tradition known as *contes de fées*, most likely derived from the Countess d'Aulnoy's book of that name, translated into English as *Tales of the Fairys* in 1699. The most famous examples from these countries are the Rhineland stories collected and domesticated by the Brothers Grimm in Germany (1812) and those transcribed from the oral tradition by Perrault in France (*Histoires ou Contes du Temps Passé* 1697). In both countries, peasant tales, from one time, were written down by bourgeois and aristocratic authors in another. Duncker says:

> The term fairy tale is now used to describe both the orally transmitted folk tales and the literary productions of bourgeois and aristocratic writers in

the late seventeenth and eighteenth century. This important distinction lies smothered under the blanket term, fairy tale; it is a split which occurred gradually in Europe, coinciding with the invention of childhood and the rise of the bourgeoisie The classical notion of ... childhood as a time of preparation and initiation into the adult world was not generally held during the Middle Ages ... Thus a radical current in popular culture was appropriated and contained ..., the tales, trapped in the anthologies by literary archaeologists like the Brothers Grimm, were captured for consumption by an educated audience and finally relegated to the nursery. (pp. 224–5)

Carter claimed to be in the 'demythologising business'. She said: 'the literary past, the myth and folklore and so on, are a vast repository of outmoded lies'. She also once said that all realist fiction from Jane Austen onwards was a collection of etiquette guides – books on morals and manners that instruct us how to behave. Carter's own fiction thus aims to strip away both the 'lies' and the 'etiquette' from traditional narrative forms.

However, if most narratives merely reinforce orthodoxies, then how does Carter subvert them? The first thing to note is her irony; the way in which all her stories are written tongue-in-cheek, a feature advertised by excessive, hyperbolic descriptions: 'my mother herself had gladly, scandalously, defiantly beggared herself for love' (ll.33–4). She further uses the fantastical and the bizarre to bring together the familiar with the unexpected, but she also always mocks and undercuts the power of fiction to enchant, to draw the reader in. In 'The Bloody Chamber', she additionally allows the new bride to tell her own story, making her an active narrator instead of a passive character in the story; and, in direct opposition to Austen, Carter's story begins, rather than ends, with marriage .

Above all, Carter uses the tools of a male literary tradition to represent both women's attraction and repulsion for patriarchal structures. These are the role models of fairy tales, the conventional positions that the stories ask readers to identify with depending on their age and gender: the single man as threatening wolf, the daughter as vulnerable innocent, her father and brothers as rescuers, and the older woman as wicked witch. In all her stories in *The Bloody Chamber*, Carter adopts the form and many of the plot elements of fairy tale but changes the roles of characters around. The grandmother becomes the wolf, the young girl is sexually predatory, or, as here, the mother becomes the rescuer, not the father. The mother in 'The Bloody Chamber' is in every respect the imperialist adventurer hero of *Boy's Own* stories, except, of course, she is a woman. Carter's story ends with mother rescuing daughter, as though from patri-archy as much as from her murderous husband.

Carter thus uses juxtaposition and pastiche to undermine the authority of existing tales. She re-works some of the conventions (even clichés) of romantic fiction; in particular, she presents the heroine of 'The Bloody Chamber' with a number of prizes: 'Mr Right', marriage, wealth, a castle in an exotic location, jewels, clothes, even a lover. Only it seems the narrator has married not for love but to 'banish the spectre of poverty from ... our meagre table' (l.32–3). Also, in this opening section, Carter toys with a convention of wedding rhetoric when the unnamed narrator considers her position between 'daughter' and 'wife', feeling a pang of loss over the fact that she is losing a mother in becoming a wife (ll.16–17). She is seduced by her roles as self-sacrificing daughter and bride, and she concentrates on the throbbing pistons, her sad mother, and her awaiting husband. The rhythm of the train is constantly mimicked in the long first sentence through exaggerated rhymes ('ecstasy of excitement'), plosive alliterations ('pressed ... pillow ... pounding ... pistons': ll.2–4), and parallel constructions ('away ... away ... away' (l.5). There is also the repetition in the opening phrases to the first two paragraphs ('I remember ... And I remember'), and the second two ('Are you sure ... Are you sure'). In every respect the narrative seems excessive, forcing the reader to pay attention to its ornate surface as much as its story.

The 'bloody chamber' itself is a locked room in the castle which her husband forbids the heroine from entering even though he gives her the key; it is also an image of genitalia (certainly, the vagina after first penetration or during menstruation; less obviously, the penis engorged with blood). The small key the Marquis insists that she must not use while he is away also suggests the key to unlock a chastity belt, illustrating one way in which Carter multiplies the generic roles that the bride is meant to take on in the story, where, without a name, she becomes representative of all past conventional heroines. Her husband is himself most easily identifiable, after Bluebeard, with the Marquis de Sade (note the importance of the French pronunciation of Mar*quis*); Carter published a book, *The Sadeian Woman*, in the same year as 'The Bloody Chamber'. Partly for this reason, the final paragraph of this opening hints at the issues of pornography, sadomasochism, and gendered desire that the rest of the story will explore. The 'domain that lay, still, beyond the grasp of my imagination' (l.50–1) is simultaneously the foam-walled 'fairy castle' to which they are headed and the 'unguessable country of marriage' (ll.6–7), or more exactly sex. The narrator is excited by her own 'young girl's' body, in anticipation of the Marquis's desire, suggested by the hint of his kisses and the teasing caress of the satin nightdress, his gift. Her initial passivity is also arguably implied by the way in which the nightdress is 'shaken loose' and then 'slipped over' her body, without her explicitly performing either action herself. The atmosphere of desire, a feeling always directed towards the future, is presaged itself in several phrases: 'voluptuously deferred', 'beyond the grasp of my imagination' and 'one day, I might'.

The extract ends by both providing a cheap thrill for the reader and, after the ridiculous phrase 'bear an heir' (l.53), grandly poking fun at the pomposity of gaudy sentiment in cheap fiction: 'Our destination, my destiny.' But Carter only establishes such hackneyed phrases and conventional gender roles in order to undermine them later in the story: the extent to which she succeeds in this is the subject of much debate.

Further Reading

Armitt, Lucie (1997) 'The fragile frames of *The Bloody Chamber*' in *The Infernal Desires of Angela Carter: Fiction, Feminity, Feminism* (ed. Joseph Bristow and Trev Lynn Broughton), Harlow: Longman.

Duncker, Patricia (1986) 'Re-Imagining the Fairy Tales: Angela Carter's Bloody Chambers' in *Popular Fictions* (ed. Peter Humm, Paul Stigart and Peter Widdowson), London: Methuen.

Gamble, Sarah (1997) *Angela Carter: Writing from the Front Line*, Edinburgh: Edinburgh University Press.

Jordan, Elaine (1992) 'The Dangers of Angela Carter' in *New Feminist Discourses* (ed. Isobel Armstrong), London: Routledge.

Chapter 23

Salman Rushdie
Shame
(1983)

In the remote border town of Q., which when seen from the air
resembles nothing so much as an ill-proportioned dumb-bell,
there once lived three lovely, and loving sisters. Their names
... but their real names were never used, like the best household
china, which was locked away after the night of their   5
joint tragedy in a cupboard whose location was eventually forgotten,
so that the great thousand-piece service from the Gardner pot-
teries in Tsarist Russia became a family myth in whose factuality
they almost ceased to believe ... the three sisters, I should state
without further delay, bore the family name of Shakil, and were   10
universally known (in descending order of age) as Chhunni,
Munnee and Bunny.
    And one day their father died.
    Old Mr Shakil, at the time of his death a widower for eighteen
years, had developed the habit of referring to the town in which   15
he lived as 'a hell hole'. During his last delirium he embarked on
a ceaseless and largely incomprehensible monologue amidst
whose turbid peregrinations the household servants could make
out long passages of obscenity, oaths and curses of a ferocity
that made the air boil violently around his bed. In this peroration 20
the embittered old recluse rehearsed his lifelong hatred for his
home town, now calling down demons to destroy the clutter of
low, dun-coloured, 'higgling' and 'piggling' edifices around the
bazaar, now annihilating with his death-encrusted words the
cool whitewashed smugness of the Cantonment district. These   25
were the two orbs of the town's dumb-bell shape: old town and
Cantt, the former inhabited by the indigenous, colonized popu-
lation and the latter by the alien colonizers, the Angrez, or
British, sahibs. Old Shakil loathed both worlds and had for
many years remained immured in his high, fortress-like, gigantic   30
residence which faced inwards to a well-like and lightless com-

158

pound yard. The house was positioned beside an open maidan,
and it was equidistant from the bazaar and the Cantt. Through
one of the building's few outward-facing windows Mr Shakil on
his death-bed was able to stare out at the dome of a large   35
Palladian hotel, which rose out of the intolerable Cantonment
streets like a mirage, and inside which were to be found golden
cuspidors and tame spider-monkeys in brass-buttoned uniforms
and bellhop hats and a full-sized orchestra playing every evening
in a stuccoed ballroom amidst an energetic riot of fantastic   40
plants, yellow roses and white magnolias and roof-high
emerald-green palms – the Hotel Flashman, in short, whose
great golden dome was cracked even then but shone nevertheless
with the tedious pride of its brief doomed glory; that dome under
which the suited-and-booted Angrez officers and white-tied   45
civilians and ringleted ladies with hungry eyes would congregate
nightly, assembling here from their bungalows to dance and to
share the illusion of being colourful – whereas in fact they were
merely white, or actually grey, owing to the deleterious effect of
that stony heat upon their frail cloud-nurtured skins, and also to 50
their habit of drinking dark Burgundies in the noonday insanity
of the sun, with a fine disregard for their lives. The old man
heard the music of the imperialists issuing from the golden hotel,
heavy with the gaiety of despair, and he cursed the hotel of
dreams in a loud, clear voice.

(London: Picador, 1984)

Before the opening sentence, *Shame* actually begins with a family
tree, to help the reader come to grips with its cast of characters but
also to signal the book's interest in genealogies and lineages, not to
say sibling rivalry, incest and nepotism. Rushdie's third novel is, he
says, a story of *universal* themes such as liberty, equality and frater-
nity (p.251), but it is also a fantastical allegory of Pakistan since its
birth, like *Shame*'s author, in 1947. This was the moment at which the
country's two halves, East and West, were split off from India at
Independence: '[a] country divided by two Wings a thousand miles
apart, that fantastical bird of a place, two Wings without a body, sun-
dered by the land-mass of its greatest foe, joined by nothing but God'
(p.178). The first sentence of *Shame* alludes to this unusual national
separation in the shape of the town of Q., which looks on the map
like 'an ill-proportioned dumb-bell'. In this it resembles the two
(dis)connected clumps of Pakistan, sticking out like misshapen ears

wrongly attached to the head of India. The mention of a 'dumb-bell' chimes with the title of this opening chapter: 'The Dumb-waiter'. The significance of these words is that this is a novel concerned with silence and the silenced – the first intimation of which occurs in the second sentence when the reader learns that the names of the three sisters are not to be revealed; we will only know their pseudonyms. Their real names are never used, locked away 'like the best house-hold china' (ll.4–5), which is the first allusion made to the fact that the sisters will remain hidden from the world, like many of the women in the book. This second sentence also gives us the image of the sisters' 'joint tragedy', the first suggestion of 'shame' in the novel (Rushdie is, however, unhappy with this translation of the Urdu 'sharam': see pp.38–9).

Rushdie's names are usually meaningful and this is the case with the surname and sobriquets of the Shakil sisters who are introduced in the first paragraph: Chhunni, Munnee and Bunny. The surname, Shakil, is one of the two major family names in the book, the other being Hyder: they are married by the union of Omar (Shamelessness) and Sufiya (Shame). Together they become a Shakil and Hyder image, the sound if not the sight of which may remind the reader of another notorious good-and-evil split-personality: Jekyll and Hyde (the motif of duality again underlines Pakistan's East and West split-personality). The three daughters' first names sound a different theme: that of colonialism. Their names end with the same sound but are all spelled differently, and this is to represent issues of language and nationality. Just as the three religions in *A Passage to India* are represented by the novel's three parts, 'Mosque', 'Caves' and 'Temple', here the different peoples are represented by the three endings -nni, -nnee, and -nny (l.11–12). These are sugges-tive of the three cultures (with their different languages) which gave birth to Pakistan, a Muslim country given Independence by a British country by tearing its two sides from the body of a Hindu country; and that is why the daughters were raised 'with the help of Parsee wet nurses, Christian ayahs, and an iron morality', the last repre-senting Muslim fundamentalism (p.13). For these reasons the novel will be concerned with division and with translation. Which brings us to the progeny of the three daughters, a son with three mothers and no known father who will be born later in the chapter and who is the novel's protagonist: Omar Khayyam. Omar sees himself as a 'translated man' (p.29), with three mother countries, too many borders, and, a peripheral place in his own life even though the nar-rator tells us he is the 'hero' of the novel (the book leans towards a negative association of change, newness or birth with mutation rather than a positive one with hybridity). That is in Chapter 1, however; Chapter 4 begins with a different protagonist: 'This is a novel about Sufiya Zinobia ... and about her surprising marriage to a certain Omar Khayyam Shakil.' Rushdie refuses to centre the novel, in terms of place or character, because this is a story about a decentred, marginalised, peripheral country, whose history and parentage has to be analysed for clues to what he sees as its 'monstrous' ill-being: 'all [Omar's] subsequent dealings with women were acts of revenge against the memory of his mothers' (p.40). Which is a good point at which to mention that, from the opening page, Rushdie is also concerned in the book with the silencing of women in Pakistan, and he attempts at various points in the narrative to rectify this in his fantastical history:

> the women seem to have taken over; they have marched in from the peripheries of the story to demand the inclusion of their own tragedies, histories and comedies, obliging me to couch my narrative in all manner of sinuous complexities, to see my 'male' plot refracted, so to speak, through the prisms of its reverse and 'female' side'. (p.173)

The clearest examples of this are the way in which Sufiya becomes a kind of demonic, avenging Beast (as called for by Old Shakil, 1.22) and in the allegorical woollen shawls embroidered by Rani Harappa (pp.191–5).

It is Omar's, which is to say Pakistan's, irregular birth that is the 'Shame' of the book's title, born of 'shameless' behaviour into the 'border' town of Q., Rushdie's version of Quetta (this shamelessness, with which Omar is born, is deemed to be inherited from the British: 'European goings-on at night that made the local tribals faint for shame': p.41). The idea of borders is so important because of the arbitrary and artificial nature of their imposition when countries or territories are mapped out, and borders are doubly important in this novel because of the creation of two Pakistans (which is one reason why the book has so many images of containment and imprisonment). Also, the creation of new borders in 1947 led to the deaths of millions of Muslims and Hindus as they passed between India and Pakistan, itself reminiscent for Muslims of the migration from Mecca of the *mohajirs*, the prophet Mohammed's followers (for example, see p.85 when Rushdie includes himself in 'we *mohajirs*'). Omar Khayyam is the name of a Persian poet chiefly famous in the West in translation, in Edward Fitzgerald's 'The Rubaiyyat of Omar Khayyam'. Twenty years after Omar's birth a brother will be born with the same triple parentage, just as Bangladesh was created (or renamed or translated) from East Pakistan 20 years after the first birth of the country.

The one-line second paragraph underlines the fact that this is to be a 'modern fairy tale' (see the discussion on pp.68–70). After the introduction of three sisters, the narrator presents a sentence which could have been taken from numerous fairy stories: 'And one day their father died.' The sentence unusually begins with 'And', as sentences in fairy tales or other oral narratives frequently do. The timeless 'one day' is also a typical phrase in mythology or folk tales, reminiscent of the 'Once upon a time' opening which was used at the start of Joyce's *A Portrait of the Artist as a Young Man* (and by Rushdie on the last page of Chapter 8). Similarly, it is unsurprising to read later in the passage that the family live in a 'high, fortress-like gigantic residence' (1.30), if not actually a castle (from which the dumb-waiter, the only access to the sisters after their father's death, will hang down like Rapunzel's hair). The idea of a fairy-tale history of Pakistan indicates Rushdie's attitude towards the modern novel, and it explains why his writing is sometimes considered magic realist or postmodernist (*Shame* is an example of what Linda Hutcheon terms 'historiographical metafiction': an interweave of story and history, literary devices and actual events). Rushdie has written that fantasy is the only mode of writing which can accommodate the modern world, which is too strange, multi-faceted, and fast-changing to be approached in any other style ('I, too, like all migrants, am a fantasist. I build imaginary countries and try to impose them on the ones that exist': p.87). This aspect is exacerbated for Western readers by Rushdie's decision to use the Hegerian calendar, putting the story in the fifteenth century, a time of romance and chivalry in the West.

The long third paragraph concerns 'Old Mr Shakil', the dying patriarch, chief of his household in the soon-to-be Pakistani town, which is still at this point part of India which is itself part of the British Empire. The dumb-bell shape of Q. is here explained in terms of colonised and coloniser, the worlds of the low 'edifices around the bazaar' of the old town and the 'cool whitewashed smugness of the Cantonment district' (1.25). They are descriptions reminiscent of the opening of *A Passage to India*. (just as the revision of English skin-colour from white to 'grey' (1.49) recalls Fielding's remark that the white races are really 'pinko-grey' in *A Passage to India*).

From the in-between border position of his house between bazaar and Cantt, Shakil 'loathed both worlds' (1.29). Also, from one of the few windows that do not face inwards to the 'well-like and lightless compound yard' (l.31) Shakil observes the Angrez dancing in the Hotel Flashman (the name of the persecuting bully in *Tom Brown's Schooldays* who went on to be a military hero of the Empire in novels by George MacDonald Fraser). The hotel represents the fading Raj, such that its 'great golden dome was cracked even then but shone nevertheless with the tedious pride of its brief doomed glory' (ll.43–4). This grandiose 20-line sentence describes the hotel as a 'mirage' (l.37) full of the pomp and show of the Raj, with its 'golden cuspidors and tame spider-monkeys in brass-buttoned uniforms' (ll.37–8) and its 'fantastic plants ... and roof-high emerald-green palms' (ll.40–2). In the stuccoed ballroom congregate three species of the Raj, each defined by one aspect of their finery: the 'suited-and-booted' military men, the 'white-tied' dignitaries and the 'ringleted' women (ll.45–6). The British Empire has often been described in terms of an illusion (l.48), and Rushdie adds to this image, depicting the end of Empire as a colourless dance in 'a stuccoed ballroom amidst an energetic riot' (l.40) of Indian colour (for example, see Hutchens, 1967). The British people 'share the illusion of being colourful' (l.48) while actually being grey and their 'noonday insanity', since only mad dogs and Englishmen go out in the midday sun, has ultimately led only to a final 'gaiety of despair' at the Empire's demise (the image is reminiscent of the story of the band still playing as the *Titanic* sank). The Raj is a 'hotel of dreams' (ll.54–5) which has lived an illusion and will give issue to the improbable two-headed offspring of Pakistan, twins *Partitioned* off from India, an enemy which was also a parent. Pakistan seems to have been, in Benedict Anderson's phrase (*Imagined Communities*, London: Verso, 1992), an 'imagined community' dreamt up by Jinnah and the British; or, to use Rushdie's own formulation in the title to his collected essays and criticism, an 'imaginary homeland'. This is underlined by the invention of the acronym 'Pakistan': 'P for the Punjabis, A for the Afghans, K for the Kashmiris, S for Sind, and the "tan", they say, for Baluchistan' (p.87). On this page the narrator goes on to conclude that the country may have failed, become self-wounding, violent and repressive, because it was 'insufficiently imagined', 'a failure of the dreaming mind', if only because the people of Bangladesh had already been left out of the name in 1947. In *Shame* Rushdie re-imagines Pakistan's history but fails to dream a better one. He names the country he has invented 'Peccavistan', after the message 'Peccavi' sent by a conquering Englishman and meaning 'I have Sind' but implying for Rushdie 'I have sinned' (p.88). The acknowledgement of this leaves shame and/or shamelessness:

'Between shame and shamelessness lies the axis upon which we turn; meteorological conditions at both these poles are of the most extreme ferocious type. Shamelessness, shame: the roots of violence' (pp.115–6). This suggests that in *Shame* Rushdie offers a new dialectic of history, in which societies swing between hedonism and puritanism, permissiveness and fundamentalism. It also returns the reader once more to the image of a split country, which, like a split personality, oscillates between shame and shamelessness, East and West (Pakistan), or simply the two heads of the dumb-bell of Q.

Further Reading

Ahmad, Aijaz (1996) *In Theory*, London: Verso.

Brennan, Timothy (1989) *Salman Rushdie and the Third World*, London: Macmillan – now Palgrave.

Hutchens, Francis (1967) *The Illusion of Permanence: British Imperialism in India*, Princeton, NJ: Princeton University Press.

Hutcheon, Linda (1988) *A Poetics of Postmodernism*, London: Routledge.

Rushdie, Salman (1991) *Imaginary Homelands: Essays and Criticism 1981–1991*, Harmondsworth: Granta.

Hanif Kureishi
The Buddha of Suburbia
(1990)

My name is Karim Amir, and I am an Englishman born and bred,
almost. I am often considered to be a funny kind of Englishman, a
new breed as it were, having emerged from two old histories. But I
don't care – Englishman I am (though not proud of it), from the
South London suburbs and going somewhere. Perhaps it is the odd   5
mixture of continents and blood, of here and there, of belonging and
not, that makes me restless and easily bored. Or perhaps it was
being brought up in the suburbs that did it. Anyway, why search the
inner room when it's enough to say that I was looking for trouble,
any kind of movement, action and sexual interest I could find,   10
because things were so gloomy, so slow and heavy, in our family, I
don't know why. Quite frankly, it was all getting me down and I was
ready for anything.

Then one day everything changed. In the morning things were
one way and by bedtime another. I was seventeen.   15

On this day my father hurried home from work not in a gloomy
mood. His mood was high, for him. I could smell the train on him as
he put his briefcase away behind the front door and took off his
raincoat, chucking it over the bottom of the banisters. He grabbed
my fleeing little brother, Allie, and kissed him; he kissed my mother   20
and me with enthusiasm, as if we'd recently been rescued from an
earthquake. More normally, he handed Mum his supper: a packet of
kebabs and chapatis so greasy their paper wrapper had disinte-
grated. Next, instead of flopping into a chair to watch the television
news and wait for Mum to put the warmed-up food on the table, he   25
went into their bedroom, which was downstairs next to the living
room. He quickly stripped to his vest and underpants.

'Fetch the pink towel,' he said to me.

I did so. Dad spread it on the bedroom floor and fell on to his
knees. I wondered if he'd suddenly taken up religion. But no, he   30
placed his arms beside his head and kicked himself into the air.

'I must practise,' he said in a stifled voice.

'Practise for what?' I said reasonably, watching him with interest
and suspicion

'They've called me for the damn yoga Olympics,' he said. He   35
easily became sarcastic, Dad.

He was standing on his head now, balanced perfectly. His
stomach sagged down. His balls and prick fell forward in his pants.
The considerable muscles in his arms swelled up and he breathed
energetically. Like many Indians he was small, but Dad was also   40
elegant and handsome, with delicate hands and manners; beside
him most Englishmen looked like clumsy giraffes. He was broad and
strong too: when young he'd been a boxer and fanatical chest-
expander. He was as proud of his chest as our next-door neighbours
were of their kitchen range. At the sun's first smile he would pull off 45
his shirt and stride out into the garden with a deckchair and a copy of
the *New Statesman*. He told me that in India he shaved his chest
regularly so its hair would sprout more luxuriantly in years to come.
I reckoned that his chest was the one area in which he'd been
forward-thinking.   50

(London: Faber, 1984)

Kureishi's semi-autobiographical novel is in the Western tradition of
Voltaire's *Candide*, a social comedy of education and growing awareness. Some critical reviews placed the narrator, Karim Amir, in the
same category of picaresque hero as protagonists in the books of the
black Americans Richard Wright, James Baldwin and Ralph Ellison
(all of whom Kureishi read avidly as a teenager), while others saw
him in terms of quintessentially English characters such as H.G.
Wells's Mr Polly or Kipps, or Kingsley Amis's Lucky Jim. From these
seemingly divergent perceptions of reviewers, the reader can begin
to consider Kureishi's novel in terms of a fusion of different types,
traditions, or ethnicities.

The hero of *The Buddha of Suburbia* grows up, first as a schoolboy
and then as an aspiring actor, against a background of 1970s popular
culture, in a world of drugs and sex populated by hippies and
punks. The book is in two halves, the first set in Kent and the second
in London and New York. Kureisihi uses the model of relocation to
indicate cultural shift, not from India to England so much as from
the suburbs to the metropolis. Fundamentally, the book rests on a
tension. On the one hand, Karim wants to be English, if 'a funny
kind of Englishman, a new breed as it were' (ll.2–3), and not at all

Indian. Until the end of the novel he will not see how he has any connections with Indian culture. On the other hand, Karim will not be allowed to be English at any point in the novel. He is therefore constantly denying and denied his position as Indian or English, but it takes most of the course of the book for him to realise that these are not either/or positions, but that he can be both English, like his mother, and Indian, like his father. Thematically, like his father's Buddhism, his difficult aim in life is to be 'balanced perfectly' (1.37). Stylistically, the conjoining of difference is expressed in the zeugma: 'delicate hands and manners', a figure of speech that brings together body and mind in the same way that Haroon aims to bring his flesh into harmony with his spirit through meditation.

Karim begins his story by announcing 'I am an Englishman born and bred, almost ... , having emerged from two old histories' (ll.2–3). Questions of belonging and hybridity pervade Kureishi's book, which in several ways concerns Karim's movement between polarised places: relocating from India to England, from England to the USA, from Orpington to West Kensington. This shifting between 'here and there' is a journey which most explicitly takes place between the two parts of the novel, entitled 'In the Suburbs' and 'In the City'.

In Part One, Karim grows up amid the thriving local scene of gauche suburban pick-and-mix appropriations of Indian culture: a series of restless characters seeking to move beyond their suburban roots through mysticism, music, class, politics and relocation. The opening concerns itself with the day 'everything changed' (1.14); when Karim's father, Haroon, comes home and starts to practise Buddhism, because he has been asked by the local Bohemians of Bromley to 'speak on one or two aspects of Oriental philosophy' (p.5). Karim's mother will not go because, significantly, 'I'm not Indian enough ... I'm only English'.

It is the sense of rootless, restless aimlessness that characterises Karim's position and fires his stated ambition that he is 'going some-where'. Karim, however, initially sees his anomie in terms of hybridity, and then suburbia: 'Perhaps it is the odd mixture of conti-nents and blood, of here and there, of belonging and not, that makes me restless and easily bored. Or perhaps it was being brought up in the suburbs that did it.' In his experience of suburbia in Kent, Karim is constantly positioned as Indian by people ranging from racists in the streets to avant-garde theatre directors. Kureishi, to an extent, characterises these as the positions of the political Right and Left. The Right feeds off a notion of Englishness which excludes all but (a minority of) Anglo-Saxon people. In the first chapters of the book, the suburban liberals also want Karim, and more particularly his father, to be genuinely 'Indian' because they see them as their shortest route to the transcendence of materialism in Bromley. In this sense, India is once more portrayed as a spiritual touchstone rather than as a country. A couple from Chislehurst epitomise this attitude by arguing that there are 'two sorts of people in the world – those who have been to India and those who haven't' (p.30). This of course would make Karim one of the second sort because he has never been to India – and neither has his father, the Buddha of suburbia, for almost 30 years. The notion of a hybrid identity, of Karim as a black English person, is constantly denied. Karim is 'an Englishman born and bred, almost' and so is constantly both abused and artificially valued for his difference, for the cultural investment that various factions have in that 'almost'.

Karim's father is also embroiled in others' stereotypical myths of Indian identity (whereas a stereotype of English culture is associated with Haroon through Karim's image of him in 'the garden with a deckchair and a copy of the *New Statesman*': ll.46–7). His incongruous position as the suburban Buddha appointed to lead those locals seeking enlightenment to a higher plane establishes the book's central attitude towards suburbia as a spiritually vacant world of materialism to be transcended or abandoned. Haroon is a British Civil Servant (a reversal of the stock-figure of the Indian Civil Servant under the Raj) but has now become an Eastern mystic in his spare time. Karim himself comments ironically on the fact that his father is supposed to be a spiritual guide but cannot even find his way around Beckenham (the stereotype of the unworldly Indian mystic). Haroon, who has spent his life becoming 'more of an Englishman' now exaggerates his accent and manner to seem more Indian when he is cast in the role of enlightener, just as Karim has to do when he is cast in the role of Kipling's Kim in a play. No less than his son, Haroon is caught between India and England, between 'here and there', between Buddhism and the suburbs. Karim's story starts with his father, as the novel's title implies, and as the events of the first page suggest. This is because he can trace his lack of interest in India directly back to his father's lack of interest:

> I did feel, looking at those strange creatures now – the Indians – that in some way these were my people, and that I'd spent my life denying or avoiding that fact. I felt ashamed and incomplete at the same time, as if half of me were missing, and as if I'd been colluding with my enemies, those whites who wanted Indians to be like them. Partly I blamed Dad for this. After all, like Anwar, for most of his life he'd never shown any

interest in going back to India. He was always honest about this: he preferred England in every way ... He wasn't proud of his past, but he wasn't unproud of it either; it just existed, and there wasn't any point in fetishizing it, as some liberals and Asian radicals like to do. So if I wanted the additional personality bonus of an Indian past, I would have to create it. (pp.212–13)

This theme of self-creation is present on the first page of the novel because Haroon, who is more physical than spiritual, is introduced as a body-builder, having been 'a boxer and fanatical chest-expander' (ll.43–4). Karim's concern with self will be somewhat different and he begins the novel 'looking for trouble, any kind of movement, action and sexual interest I could find' (ll.9–10). Only later will he be able to answer his own question, 'why search the inner room' (ll.8–9), and consider his identity in relation to his ethnicity and the politics of (re)location.

One reason for this introspection is that events in the second half of the novel have increased Karim's political awareness, and just as the opening of the novel is on a day 'everything changed' (l.14), its end is at another key moment: 'England's had it ... Resistance has brought it to a standstill. The Government were defeated in the vote last night. There'll be an election ... It's either us or the rise of the Right.' (p.258). The last day of the novel is the day of Margaret Thatcher's Conservative Party election in 1979, at the end of the Labour period of office, the end of the counter-cultural movements of the 1960s and 1970s, and at the end of Karim's story. But it is also the start of his reflections, the point at which he will begin writing the story we have just read, as he can finally answer his own initial question of 'why search the inner room' (ll.8–9), and 'think about the past and what I'd been through as I'd struggled to *locate* myself' (pp.283–4; my emphasis).

Further Reading

Ball, John Clement (1996) 'The Semi-Detached Metropolis: Hanif Kureishi's London', *Ariel*, 27:4 (October).

Childs, Peter (1998) 'Hanif Kureishi' in *British Novelists Since 1960* (ed. Merritt Moseley), Detroit, MI: Gale.

Kaleta, Kenneth C. (1998) *Hanif Kureishi: Postcolonial Storyteller*, Austin: University of Texas

Kureishi, Hanif (1986) 'The Rainbow Sign' in *My Beautiful Laundrette and The Rainbow Sign*, London: Faber & Faber.

Glossary

(This glossary includes useful critical terms which will be encountered but not explained elsewhere in the book.)

ALLITERATION
Repeated rhyming consonant sounds. For example, the 'r' sounds in 'Around the rocks the rugged rascal ran'.

ALLUSION
An overt or indirect reference to something else, whether a text, person, event or anything else.

ASSONANCE
Repeated rhyming vowel sounds. For example, the 'oo' sounds in 'You do not woo at the zoo.'

BALLAD
A poem, composed for singing, that narrates a story, usually dramatic. A traditional ballad, passed down from generation to generation by word of mouth, typically has a simple verse structure, refrains, stock phrases, repetitions, dialogue, and an impersonal narrator. A literary ballad is a work written in imitation of the traditional ballad.

BILDUNGSROMAN
A German word that translates as 'novel [*Roman*] of development [*Bildungs*]'. It is associated with novels that show an individual coming of age or serving some kind of apprenticeship. Its main theme is therefore usually the protagonist's growth or development from childhood to adulthood. Classic examples are Dickens's *David Copperfield*, Mark Twain's *Huckleberry Finn*, and Charlotte Brontë's *Jane Eyre*.

DIALOGISM
Dialogism is the Russian critic M. M. Bakhtin's term for the way in which meaning is constructed out of the contending discourses within any culture, such that there is continual interaction and struggle between different meanings. No discourse or word exists in

a vacuum: everything has meaning in relation to other things, and so is part of a larger whole. Fiction is inherently dialogic, because (in direct contrast to a form like the lyric) its very nature is to orchestrate a number of different voices, including a narrator's. What we call truth is something born 'between' these voices, and never fully grown. Dialogue is always open-ended, and never finalised; so is truth. This is crucial to Bakhtin: discourse never comes to an end and is always unfinished. Each utterance takes place in response to, and in anticipation of, something else, and this process is unending. (See also the entry on Heteroglossia)

ELLIPSIS
A gap in the text usually indicated by three dots. An ellipsis requires the reader either to reconcile themselves to the omission, and conjecture on its importance, or to speculate on what has been repressed: what has gone unsaid or un-narrated. It is a technique used extensively by some fiction writers (such as Katherine Mansfield) and hardly ever by others.

FIGURE OF SPEECH
An unusual use of language, almost invariably non-literal and often used to associate or compare unconnected things. The best known figures of speech are metaphor, metonymy, personification, simile and synecdoche. (See entries on these terms below)

FRAME NARRATION
An introductory, and often also concluding, narration which frames the chief narration. The main story, by a second but principal narrator, is usually embedded in the first narrator's account (for instance, *Wuthering Heights*, where the first narrator, Lockwood, delivers without speech marks the words, 'a little condensed' (p.155), of the principal narrator, Nelly; or *Heart of Darkness*, where the long narrative of the principal narrator, Marlow, is reported as speech within that of the first narrator). However, the first narrator may simply lead up to the central story and then offer no further comment (for example, *The Turn of the Screw*).

FREE INDIRECT DISCOURSE
The representation of speech or thought without tags (such as 'he said' or 'she thought') or quotation marks. Speech with quotation marks is considered 'direct' and that without 'indirect'. Therefore, there are four possible ways of representing the same piece of speech:

'I have come to believe that he will leave,' she said. (Tagged direct discourse)

'I have come to believe that he will leave.' (Free direct discourse)

She had come to believe that he would leave, she said. (Tagged indirect discourse)

She had come to believe that he would leave. (Free indirect discourse)

GENRE

The three major genres of literature are poetry, prose fiction and drama, but there are many subgenres such as Gothic, satire, tragedy, comedy, the *Bildungsroman*, the picaresque, the ode and the sonnet.

GOTHIC

The Gothic novel is a subgenre of fiction usually considered to have been initiated by Horace Walpole's *The Castle of Otranto* (1764). Some of the subgenre's characteristics are a gloomy setting, dark mysteries, an atmosphere of foreboding, simplistically good or evil characters, passionate natures, remote locations, and graphic or implied horror. Its heyday continued until the 1820s, but novels and films in the Gothic mode still appear regularly. Mary Shelley's *Frankenstein* is in the Gothic vein, and Angela Carter's 'The Bloody Chamber' is in part a pastiche of it.

HETEROGLOSSIA

The Russian critic M. M. Bakhtin's use of 'heteroglossia' (from the Greek, meaning 'other tongues') expresses the belief that all utterances contain the traces of other utterances and that there are always a number of competing languages at work at any one time, even within one speech. Bakhtin, for example, in 'Discourse in the novel' in *The Dialogic Imagination* analyses passages of Dickens to show that the characters' speech is not only ideologically saturated but is a mix of all sorts of different discourses: religious (expressions from the Bible), political (pronouncements on social reform), moral, legalistic, colloquial, and so on. While Bakhtin uses the term 'polyphony' to describe many voices working at once, heteroglossia describes many discourses at work in any one of those voices. It both expresses this linguistic diversity embedded in any utterance and expresses the plurality of relations in all utterances. Heteroglossia is most fundamentally a name for the perception that the world is made up of a large number of antagonistic languages. (See also the entry on Dialogism)

INTERPELLATION

A political theory of the construction of the subject formulated by the Marxist critic Louis Althusser and summarised as 'all ideology hails or interpellates concrete individuals as concrete subjects'. Ideology and language attempt to create a new representation or belief in the consciousness of the 'individual' who, in (mis)recognising her or his image in discourse, takes up a subject-position (assumes an 'identity'). Everyone is therefore constantly interpellated or 'called' into a particular cultural position by discourses of gender, class, ethnicity, sexuality, and so on.

INTERTEXTUALITY
Though often employed as a synonym for allusion, reference or echo, intertextuality refers to the belief that all texts are made up of citations, are (in effect) weaves of other texts.

IRONY
A term in rhetoric to signal a gap between word and meaning, between what is said and what is meant or conveyed.

LINEAR PLOT
A plot that proceeds chronologically, without extended flashbacks or significant atemporal ordering of events in the narrative. This is the most common way of recounting a story, but modernist novels, in particular, frequently eschew the use of linear narrative.

METAFICTION
Self-conscious, self-reflexive fiction which draws attention to its own methods of construction. In the critic Patricia Waugh's words, this is 'fiction which calls attention to itself as an artifact in order to raise questions about the relationship between fiction and reality'.

METAPHOR and METONYMY
Figures of speech. Metaphor works by substituting one word or image for another in terms of resemblance (for example, the Latin phrase *tempus fugit* is still used frequently today in its English translation of 'Time flies', not because it literally does but because it often appears to elapse quickly). By contrast, metonymy works by contiguity and association, and replaces an object with its attribute ('the deep' instead of 'the sea'). Metonymy is often considered also to include synecdoche (see below).

MIMESIS and DIEGESIS
Mimesis is a word used by Plato in *The Republic* to describe the imitative representation of speech. By contrast, *diegesis* is the term he uses to indicate when 'the poet himself is the speaker and does not even attempt to suggest to us that anyone but himself is speaking'. In narrative, diegesis is distinguished from mimesis to describe the way

narrators indirectly report and summarise speech or scenes (telling) rather than presenting them directly through monologue, dialogue or direct speech (showing). Aristotle, in his *Poetics*, expands *mimesis* to include the 'imitation of an action' as well as the representation of speech.

MODERNISM

The vast majority of attempts to offer alternative modes of representation to *realism* from the middle of the nineteenth century to the middle of the twentieth century have at one time or another been termed Modernist, and this applies to literature, music, painting, film and architecture (and to some works before and after this period). In poetry, Modernism is associated with moves to break from the iambic pentameter as the basic unit of verse to introduce *vers libre* (free verse), symbolism and other new forms of writing. In prose, Modernism is associated with attempts to render human subjectivity in ways more real than realism: to represent consciousness, perception, emotion, meaning and the individual's relation to society through, among other tools, interior monologue, stream of consciousness, defamiliarisation, rhythm and irresolution. Modernist writers therefore struggled, in Ezra Pound's brief phrase, to 'make it new', to modify if not overturn existing modes of representation, partly by pushing them towards the abstract or the introspective, and to express the new sensibilities of their time: in a compressed, condensed, complex literature of the city, of industry and technology, war, machinery and speed, mass markets and communication, of internationalism, the New Woman, the aesthete, the nihilist and the flâneur.

OEDIPUS/ELECTRA COMPLEX

According to Freud, a number of largely unconscious feelings in the under-five child focusing on the wish to possess the parent of the opposite sex and overthrow the parent of the same sex.

PATHETIC FALLACY

An expression coined by the critic and essayist John Ruskin in 1856 in *Modern Painters* to describe the way inanimate nature may be endowed with human emotions in art. One of Ruskin's examples is Kingsley's 'cruel, crawling foam' in *Alton Locke*. Another example would be Forster's line in the opening of *A Passage to India*: 'when the sky chooses, glory can rain into the Chandrapore bazaars'.

PERSONIFICATION

Personification is a trope, or figure of speech, in which human characteristics are attributed to animals, deities, nature, or something inanimate or abstract. ('Anthropomorphism' is the general term used when something non-human is treated in human terms and 'animism' refers to any description in which something that cannot move itself is animated.) Examples from common expressions would be 'blind faith', 'trembling leaves' or 'angry sky'. See also 'Pathetic Fallacy', which applies only to 'inanimate nature'.

PICARESQUE

From the Spanish *picaro*, an unpleasant anti-social character of low birth in sixteenth-century novels. In English literature *picaresque* has come to mean a rambling, episodic story with a narrator or hero from the lower classes. Novels discussed in terms of this subgenre are: Defoe's *Moll Flanders*, Fielding's *Tom Jones* and Dickens's *Nicholas Nickleby*.

PROLEPSIS

A figure of speech in which a future event is treated as though it has happened or is happening. (See the introduction for a longer discussion)

READERLY and WRITERLY

Terms coined by the French cultural and literary critic Roland Barthes in *S/Z* to distinguish between the way 'classic realist' texts, which he called 'readerly', can encourage their passive consumption by conforming to familiar narrative codes (for example, of coherence, linear structure, clear plot, strong characterisation and historical specificity), and experimental 'writerly' texts disrupt those codes and so place a greater weight on the reader's active participation in the construction of the text's meanings.

REALISM

Realism, according to many critics, is characterised by its attempt objectively to offer up a mirror to the world, thus disavowing its own culturally conditioned processes and ideological stylistic assumptions. Realism, modelled on prose forms such as history and journalism, generally features characters, language, and a spatial and temporal setting very familiar to its contemporary readers, and often presents itself as transparently representative of the author's society. The hegemony of realism was challenged by Modernism and then postmodernism, as alternative ways of representing reality and the world. Realism itself was once a new, innovative form of writing, with authors such as Daniel Defoe (1660–1731) and Samuel Richardson (1690–1761) providing a different template for fiction from the previously dominant mode of prose writing, the Romance, which was parodied in one of the very first novels, Cervantes' *Don Quixote* (1605–15), and survives in Gothic and fantasy fiction. Throughout modern literary history, realism remains the favourite style of writing for novelists. 'Classic realism', which flowered in the nineteenth century, has been delineated by critics such as Roland Barthes, Colin MacCabe and Catherine Belsey. It is a term used to describe the work of such writers as Balzac, Dickens, Mrs Gaskell, and George Eliot: novels with reliable narrators who deal with con-temporary social and political problems. David Lodge provides this summary in *After Bakhtin* (London: Routledge, 1990: 26):

> The mode of classic realism with its concern for coherence and causality in narrative structure, for the autonomy of the individual self in the presentation of character, for a readable homogeneity and urbanity of style, is equated with liberal humanism, with empiricism, common sense and the presentation of bourgeois culture as a kind of nature.

REALITY EFFECT

A term coined by the French literary and cultural critic Roland Barthes in *The Rustle of Language*. Barthes observes a kind of 'aesthetic verisimilitude' in realist writers which is not denotative but connotative: descriptive details are not mere scene-setting, structurally superfluous notations used to *depict* reality, but are constructed to conform to conventions of representation and therefore to *signify* reality ('the reality effect').

ROMANCE

A subgenre that has its origin in medieval literature. First used to describe verse narratives about knights and heroes on a quest. The best known example in English is probably *Sir Gawain and the Green Knight*, which dates from 1375. From the latter part of the eighteenth century, a romance is a story in which the scenes and incidents are surrounded by an atmosphere of strangeness and mystery. The Romance involves heroes, the supernatural, symbols and adventure. Romance aims at the embodiment of psychic or moral truths which cannot be expressed through a depiction of everyday reality. It is therefore concerned with unreal or fantastic worlds in order to deal with the beliefs, principles and ethical systems that lie behind human behaviour but which are not necessarily evident if we simply observe what people do.

SIGNIFIER/SIGNIFIED

For the Swiss linguist Ferdinand de Saussure, the signifier and signified are the two sides to the linguistic sign, which previously had been considered to be made up of 'a word' and 'a thing'. The signifier refers to the sound image or written mark used to represent an abstract concept or idea, the signified. For Saussure the two were inseparable despite the relation between them being arbitrary.

SIMILE
A particular kind of metaphor which works by direct comparison using the words 'like' or 'as'. For example: 'My love is like a red, red rose.'

SPATIAL READING
The idea that every part of a text has to be considered in the light of the knowledge of every other part. The complex construction of many texts militates against drawing conclusions from any part of them in isolation.

SYNECDOCHE
A figure of speech in which a part is used to represent the whole. For example, Dickens refers to the workers repeatedly as 'hands' in *Hard Times*. Synecdoche also works by substituting the whole for the part (as in 'Scotland played hockey last night').

UNRELIABLE NARRATOR
A narrator who does not properly comprehend the world and whose judgements the reader mistrusts.

VERISIMILITUDE
The appearance or semblance of truth to nature or reality.

Index